D0849175

MARCUS AURELIUS

, , ,

THE EMPEROR'S HANDBOOK

A New Translation of the *Meditations*

, , ,

C. Scot Hicks

AND

David V. Hicks

SCRIBNER

New York   London   Toronto   Sydney   Singapore

SCRIBNER
1230 Avenue of the Americas
New York, NY 10020

SCRIBNER and design are trademarks of Macmillan Library Reference USA, Inc.,
used under license by Simon & Schuster, the publisher of this work.

For information about special discounts for bulk purchases,
please contact Simon & Schuster Special Sales:
1-800-465-6798 or business@simonandschuster.com

DESIGNED BY ERICH HOBBING

Text set in Adobe Garamond

Manufactured in the United States of America

1   3   5   7   9   10   8   6   4   2

Library of Congress Cataloging-in-Publication Data
Marcus Aurelius, Emperor of Rome, 121–180.
[Meditations. English]
The emperor's handbook : a new translation of the Meditations /
C. Scot Hicks and David V. Hicks
p.   cm.
Includes index.
1. Ethics. 2. Stoics. 3. Life.
I. Hicks, C. Scot, 1954– II. Hicks, David V. III. Title.
B580 .H53 M3713 2002
188—dc21   2002075232

ISBN 0-7432-3383-2

For our parents

CONTENTS

THE EMPEROR'S
HANDBOOK

INTRODUCTION

The book you are about to read was never intended for publication, whatever that might have meant in the second century. It is often referred to as the *Meditations* of the Emperor Marcus Aurelius, but in fact it was untitled in antiquity and takes the form of notes intended for personal and private use. How these notes ever got into our hands is one of those tantalizing mysteries that historical novels are made of.

Did the emperor write his notes on fragile papyrus or portable wax tablets? When, under the grueling conditions of camp life on the Roman frontier, did he find time to jot down his thoughts? Was it a daily routine, or whenever he could grab a moment? Or was there a scribe? Might Marcus have dictated such probing and introspective, yet strangely impersonal notes?

When he died, probably from exhaustion after thirteen years of grinding warfare with the Germans, did he leave instructions for the safekeeping of his notes? Did he entrust them to a friend, a relative, a fellow Stoic? Or in the confusion of the moment, were they discovered by a servant and spirited away and later sold for bread? Did the captain of his guard requisition them with everything else on the emperor's person at the time of his death and turn them over to the imperial family or a Senate in mourning? And after that, by what circuitous and utterly silent route did they end up in the hands of an aristocratic Byzantine humanist and scholar during the reign of Leo the Wise?

This much we surmise. Sometime before his election as bishop of Caesarea (Cappadocia) in 907, a Byzantine scholar and churchman named Arethas sent a letter to Demetrios, the metropolitan of Heraclea in Pontus, presenting him with what he described as "the most useful old book of the Emperor Marcus." All our fourteenth- and fifteenth-century manuscripts are thought to derive from this book, or the copy Arethas made of it before giving it away.

What is far clearer is the progress of Marcus Aurelius' book since the Renaissance. The attentions of humanists after the fall of Byzantium, of scholars Meric Casaubon (who made the first English translation) and Thomas Gataker (who created the chapter divisions still in use) in the seventeenth century, of essayist Matthew Arnold and historian Ernst Renan in the nineteenth century, and of statesmen and scholars in the twentieth century have ensured for Marcus' words a profound and worldwide influence. In our own time, public figures as far apart on the political spectrum as Admiral James Stockdale and President Bill Clinton have praised the emperor's book, and the historian Michael Grant has called it "one of the most acute and sophisticated pieces of ancient writing that exists" and, "incidentally, the best book ever written by a major ruler."

The Purpose of the Book

At the end of the tenth century, a Byzantine lexicon known as the *Souda* cited several passages from a work by Marcus the philosopherking organized in twelve books and described as "the regimen of his personal life." We have not tampered with this arrangement. Except for the first book, which may have been written last and reads like an author's acknowledgments, all the books are alike. There is no beginning, middle, or ending. The reader can pick up and start anywhere, and thoughts that appear in the second book will reappear in different garb in later books. This pattern is consistent with the observation that we need more often to be reminded than informed.

From notes inserted between the first and second and between the second and third books, it appears that Marcus wrote *The Emperor's Handbook* during the last years of his life while camped with his army along the frozen marshes of the Danube. Yet this is not a diary. Marcus almost never refers to what is happening in camp or in the rest of the empire. He is concerned exclusively with his own thoughts, although not in a systematic or speculative way. This is not a philosophical treatise. Marcus' thoughts appear to emerge from an inner dialogue that is as relentless as it is rooted in the loamy soil of daily life.

The arrangement and content of *The Emperor's Handbook* suggest that it was written as a series of thought exercises consistent with a discipline encouraged by Stoics like Seneca and Epictetus, and out of which later grew the Christian practice of spiritual exercises. Marcus labored over the expression of his thoughts and gave them many forms. Sometimes he records them as a dialogue with himself; sometimes he poses a question or berates himself; sometimes he tells a joke or quotes something he has read; but always, he is reminding himself of a Stoic precept that will help him act reasonably and in harmony with nature. Whether creating or copying, he is like a carpenter working a fine piece of furniture. Each piece needs not only to serve a purpose, but to do so boldly, beautifully, memorably. This accounts for the striking and often aphoristic way Marcus addresses himself.

> Know that in time those things toward which we move come to be. (VI.50)

> Bear in mind that the measure of a man is the worth of the things he cares about. (VII.3)

> Leave the wrong with the person who did it. (VII.29)

Through regular mental exercise of this sort, Marcus sought to furnish his mind with true, good, and beautiful things. Someone with a mind so furnished, he believed, must *do* true, good, and beautiful things, since action follows thought. "Your mind," he wrote (V.16), "is colored by the thoughts it feeds upon, for the mind is dyed by ideas and imaginings. Saturate your mind, then, with a succession of ideas like these . . ." and he proceeds to remind himself of the ideas that will make it possible for him "to live in a palace in the right way." As important as the form of his ideas is their usefulness. They are, after all, furniture.

> When your spirits need a lift, think of the virtues and talents of those around you—one's energy, another's modesty, the generosity of a third, something else in a fourth. Nothing is so inspiring or uplifting as the sight of these splendid qualities in our friends. Keep them always in mind. (VI.48)

Everything about *The Emperor's Handbook* suggests that Marcus used it to remind himself of his guiding principles and to hold himself accountable to them. These are not merely thoughts "recollected in tranquillity," but they contain the landmarks and lighthouses by which he navigated a life, the life not of a saintly recluse, but of a general, administrator, legislator, husband, father, and judge besieged on all sides. For this reason, we have titled his notes a "handbook" and have taken the liberty allowed by a modern translation of an ancient text (designed for oral rather than visual presentation) to highlight some of Marcus' more memorable and apt aphorisms.

Like thousands of other English-speaking people who are reasonably well educated, we have enjoyed reading Marcus over the years and marveled at the ability of someone so far removed from us in language, time, culture, creed, and station in life to know so much about us and to offer such pertinent advice. At the same time, we wondered at the awkwardness of his English translators and knew enough Greek to know that his Greek was not that bad, although some have claimed it was. We resolved to rectify this situation, and in the process, we hoped to make the provocative wisdom of this extraordinary man available to a wider audience. It is fine for scholars to study Marcus, but it is *natural* for the captains of industries and armies to carry him in their briefcases, for this was a man of action, not merely of words, and the few words he wrote to himself were meant to incite actions, not dissertations.

"It's Up to You!"

Scholars interested in Marcus' ideas typically argue over whether he is a consistent Stoic and criticize him for being unoriginal or unsystematic in his thinking. But their debate largely misses the point. Marcus has little interest in ideas for their own sake. He wants ideas that prove their usefulness in helping him to live a happier, more purposeful and productive life. He constantly cautions himself to disregard ideas that are "indifferent," that are of no practical, moral, or social benefit. This does not mean that he disregards poetry and physics, religion and the arts. It means he bores into these subjects to extract and apply their meanings to the question of how to live and manage the affairs of the empire.

Marcus sounds this theme right from the beginning. In Book One, he reserves his thanks and praise for those who taught him how to live and govern others well, and he seems strangely silent or reserved in commenting on the contributions of teachers like Herodes Atticus and Fronto, his famous Greek and Latin tutors. He thanks the gods "for not letting my education in rhetoric, poetry, and other literary subjects come easily to me, and thereby sparing me from an absorbing interest in these subjects" (I.17). If that is not enough, he concludes the introduction to his thoughts with a word of guidance from the oracle at Caieta that seems to summarize what he has learned from an astoundingly active and challenging life: "It's up to you!" (I.17).

As every school boy and girl used to know, Marcus was the last of the "five good emperors." Born in 121, he died fighting the German tribes in 180 at the age of fifty-eight. He ruled Rome at the height of its power and was, in many ways, the fabulous realization of Plato's dream of a philosopher-king. The contemporary historian Dio Cassius called his rule an age of gold. Trajan had crossed the Danube and added Dacia (Romania) to the empire and later marched his armies all the way to the Red Sea. Hadrian had walled the unruly Celts out of Britannia, and Antoninus Pius had moved his wall deeper into Celtic territory. Spain and Africa had yielded to the sword and were prospering under the plow. Cities in Greece, Italy, and Gaul flourished under Roman law and were joined by a network of aqueducts and roads that undergird the infrastructure of Southern Europe to this day. Never again would civilization reach these heights under one ruler.

Marcus himself seemed impossibly good. His father died when he was three years old, and his mother and grandfather Verus (meaning "true" or "sincere") raised him. As a boy, he was universally admired for his serious demeanor and friendly disposition. Even the aged emperor Hadrian, visiting in his grandfather's home, marked him as destined to rule and was so taken with and perhaps amused by the child's *gravitas* and noble bearing that he playfully nicknamed him

"Verissimus" ("truest" or "most earnest"), a nickname that stuck and later appeared on coins. Untainted by the incalculable wealth and absolute power that had corrupted many of his notorious predecessors, this boy grew to manage one of the most complex enterprises of all time in the midst of personal and geopolitical catastrophes, any one of which would have undone most men.

In 138 Hadrian died, and in accordance with his wishes, the new emperor, Antoninus Pius, adopted Marcus. In the same year Marcus was betrothed to Pius' daughter Faustina, whom he married in 145. Was it a happy marriage? It is hard to say. Marcus adored Faustina, although rumors of her infidelities swirled around the palace. In Marcus' notes he describes her as sweet, affectionate, and unassuming. She bore him at least fourteen children, but the only son to survive was Commodus, Marcus' vain and unstable successor, later rumored, perhaps because his character bore so little resemblance to his father's, to be "the gift of a gladiator." Yet in spite of all the pain and embarrassment it must have caused him, Marcus loved his family and appears to have spent as much time in their company as his imperial duties allowed.

Antoninus Pius provided Marcus with the best private tutors power and money could buy. These included the two most famous orators of the age. Herodes Atticus, his Greek tutor and perhaps the richest man in the Eastern Empire, personally financed the Odeon that still graces the slopes of the Acropolis in Athens. Marcus' lifelong correspondence with Marcus Cornelius Fronto, his Latin tutor, also survives and offers us many insights into the emperor and his times. Yet for all their influence and friendship, Marcus rejected oratory as a vain and empty occupation, and not unlike Alexander, the student of Aristotle, he embraced the active life, partly, it must be said, from a sense of duty. This was, after all, his fate as an emperor, and it is an axiom of his leadership philosophy that one must accept one's fate without reservation or complaint.

Marcus assumed the title of Caesar in 139, became consul in 140, and was invested with tribunician power from 147 to 161 when Antoninus Pius died. In effect, he ruled with Pius during these years while being mentored by his adoptive father. At the death of Pius, Marcus Aurelius became emperor and promptly named as co-emperor Lucius Ceionius Commodus, now called Lucius Verus, whom Pius had adopted at the same time as Marcus, perhaps out of respect for Hadrian's wishes. Why did Marcus do this? There was no precedent in Rome for co-emperors, although this action established one, and Lucius Verus does not appear to have figured in Pius' succession plans. Moreover, Lucius was a playboy and, like Marcus' later son also named Commodus, notably lacking in leadership ability.

The answer must be that, having ruled with Pius for roughly two decades, Marcus felt the burden of office was too great for one man to bear. He regarded his own health as precarious, and since he had no heirs at this time, he may also have felt he was buying insurance for the empire with this move. At any rate, he seems to have had real affection for and no illusions about his brother by adoption. The arrangement worked because Lucius deferred to Marcus, and Marcus surrounded him with capable men. One of the recurring themes in Marcus' handbook is leadership's responsibility to work intelligently with what it is given and not waste time fantasizing about a world of flawless people and perfect choices.

Now, the calm characterizing the reigns of Hadrian and Antoninus Pius suddenly ended. Famine and floods struck Italy; there were earthquakes in Asia; and the army in Britannia revolted. More threatening than these, the vast Parthian empire attacked Syria and replaced the friendly king of Armenia with a man hostile to Rome. Lucius was sent east to deal with this threat, and his generals, carefully selected by Marcus, prevailed. But out of this success came an even worse disaster. The army returned with a plague. Scholars estimate that the plague killed off as many as a third of those living in the empire at the time, decimating the army, where whole legions were wiped out, destroying the tax base and exhausting the treasury, emptying the countryside, causing massive food shortages, and undermining the empire's self-confidence.

No sooner were the Parthians subdued and the traditional triumph celebrated in Rome than land-hungry German tribes, pushed south by the Goths descending from the Baltic, began to invade the empire. Both Lucius and Marcus traveled north with the army to meet this new threat, but Lucius died of a stroke in his carriage on the way, and Marcus returned to Rome with his body. He would now govern Rome until his death, alone. Most of the last thirteen years of his life he spent campaigning against the Germans on the northern frontier in and around modern Hungary. In the midst of it all, his general in the east, Avidius Cassius, possibly plotting with his wife, Faustina, declared himself emperor. This forced Marcus to break off a promising campaign against the Germans and to march east to quell the rebellion. Before he had gone far a centurion brought him Cassius' head, which he famously declined to look upon while expressing regret at having been denied the pleasure of pardoning the usurper. He had all the correspondence burned, presumably to protect Cassius' co-conspirators as well as the reputation of Faustina, who died soon thereafter and was sincerely mourned by her husband.

Although never strong physically, and perhaps even sickly, Marcus worked hard all day, pausing to eat only at night, and then only a little. Fantastically conscientious, he never did anything, not even the smallest thing, as if he considered it unimportant. He took a detailed interest in all matters arising from his military and administrative responsibilities, and he judged others and made his appointments, with the two puzzling exceptions named Commodus, strictly on merit. Americans, accustomed to think in terms of separation of powers and therefore of duties, civilian and military, executive, legislative, judicial, and so on, may have difficulty comprehending the range of powers and responsibilities of a Roman emperor. As a judge, for example, Marcus raised the number of court days in a year to two hundred and thirty, and his verdicts were as meticulous as they often were merciful. He carried his leadership principle—"It's up to you!"—into all areas of responsibility.

Marcus lived and governed, perhaps more than any powerful man ever has, by his own precepts. As his handbook attests, he regarded obstacles as opportunities for the exercise of reason, or for what we might call "creative problem-solving." He refused to see a life crowded with calamities as ill-starred, and viewed it instead as a natural and welcome test of his mind and guiding principles. He believed, as we would say these days, that leaders must be "inner directed," and he reserved some of his most lively invective for pundits and popular opinion. One never finds his wetted finger in the air. He disliked gladiatorial spectacles, for instance, and caused a shortage of gladiators by conscripting them into the army, and he invited further criticism by requiring them to use blunted swords in the circus. Rather than tax citizens already impoverished by the plague, he sold the imperial flatware and his wife's jewelry and dresses to finance the German wars. Yet when he learned that an earthquake had destroyed the beautiful city of Smyrna in Asia Minor, he wept openly and ordered it rebuilt at public expense.

This was the man who died with his army on the banks of the Danube two months short of his fifty-ninth birthday and left behind a thin sheaf of notes that speak to the soul of anyone who has ever exercised authority or faced adversity or believed in a better day. His watchword—"It's up to you!"—is the irreducible attitude of the leader, the person who assumes responsibility for the outcome in whatever situation he finds himself. *The Emperor's Handbook* is written to a person with this attitude, and in much of it, Marcus seeks to discern between those outcomes for which he is truly responsible and those which are beyond his control. This discernment is important to the leader, who must husband his energies, prioritize his efforts, and remain poised and positive in the face of challenges before which he is sometimes powerless.

Thoughts That Lead to Action

Two obstacles stand between us and a fair, much less a sympathetic, reading of Marcus. They both pertain to our modern conception of freedom. First, we tend to conceive of freedom, even the religious freedoms we take pretty much for granted, in largely political terms, perhaps because, second, we have come seriously to doubt our psychological freedom, or freedom of mind. Consequently, we think of our actions as having causes outside the mind or buried deep in sub-consciousness and beyond the reach of reasoned thought and dialogue.

On the one hand, Marcus thanks his brother Severus for "the idea of a state in which all men are equal under the law and free to say what they think, and of an empire that respects above all else the liberty of its subjects" (I.14). But this is his only mention of what we would call political freedom, and to a modern ear, it must sound strange coming from an emperor whose laws tended to favor the ruling class (*honestiores*) over the common people (*humiliores*), who himself increased the distinctions between citizens and non-citizens, and who continued the policy of suppressing Christianity. Perhaps here Marcus is giving lip service to an ideal that he felt was unachievable, human nature being what it is. Unachievable, but still worth striving for.

On the other hand, references to freedom sound like a *basso continuo* throughout the *Handbook*.

> Although others may at times hinder me from acting, they cannot control or impede my spirit and my will. Reserving its judgments and adapting to change, my mind bypasses or displaces any obstacles in its way. It uses whatever opposes it to achieve its own ends; it turns roadblocks into roads. (V.20)

> There is no reason why you shouldn't live here on earth as you'd like to live in the hereafter. If others won't permit it, then it's time to call it quits and exit this life with grace and equanimity. "The chimney smokes; I'm leaving the room." Why make more of it than that? But as long as nothing drives me from the room, I'm a free man, and no one can keep me from living as I like, which is to conform to the nature of a reasonable and sociable being. (V.29)

It came down to Marcus' belief that we are what we think and desire. From our thoughts and desires spring our actions. Doing follows thinking. Our freedom begins in our thinking, not in our doing. When we control what we think and desire, only then are we free. Those who fail to grasp this live in chains. They may be *politically* free to say or do what they like, but their thoughts and desires are out of their control, or more precisely, their irrational and antisocial thoughts and desires enslave them.

Firmly convinced of this, Marcus dwells insistently on considerations of how to guard the mind from false opinions and harmful desires. He reminds us that we are bombarded by sensations received through our five senses and by the observations and opinions of others. Yet none of this is real for us until our minds acknowledge or accept it. We have the power to ignore sensory data and to dismiss or reserve judgment about cognitive data.

> Treat with utmost respect your power of forming opinions, for this power alone guards you against making assumptions that are contrary to nature and judgments that overthrow the rule of reason. It enables you to learn from experience, to live in harmony with others, and to walk in the way of the gods. (III.9)

If we fail to exercise this power of self-censorship and judgment, either out of mental laziness or from the conviction that this power is illusory, then we are the adman's dream, and our lives are not our own. The self-seeking politician, drunk with power, manipulates us. Our political freedoms become trivialized in the process, and we grow cynical about the only freedom we claim to possess.

The conviction that we are what we think ought to change our feelings about others as well. The issue is no longer what others do, but what thought processes lead them to do it. Our understanding of their thoughts will probably change how we feel about them and what they have done.

> When someone wrongs you, ask yourself: what made him do it? Once you understand his concept of good and evil, you'll feel sorry for him and cease to be either amazed or angry. If his concept is similar to yours, then you are bound to forgive him since you would have acted as he did in similar circumstances. But if you do not share his ideas of good and evil, then you should find it even easier to overlook the wrongs of someone who is confused and in a moral muddle. (VII.26)

Likewise, our charged emotional lives flow between the positive and negative poles of desire: the desire to possess and its opposite, fear, the desire to avoid. What should we desire and fear in order not to be the slave of either emotion? Marcus' responses to this question contribute, no doubt, to the popular image of the Stoic as one who is indifferent to pleasure and pain, unafraid of death, resigned to his fate, and welcomes adversity as an ally in the lifelong struggle for moral improvement. Although far from complete, this is not an inaccurate picture, and we are tempted to dismiss the case before hearing it because we do not like the verdict. Suffice it to say, many find it a harder case to dismiss after they have heard it.

Now, if a free mind begins to sound like common sense, it is important to remember the extent to which Marcus' confidence in the mind's freedom to choose its guiding principles, to suppress desire, and to enforce rational behavior is misplaced in today's world. Modern philosophers and social scientists have used their minds to dismiss the mind. Ignoring the logical contradiction in their doing so, they reject, or at least place disabling restrictions upon, the idea that we are free to think. The mind is no longer the originator of ideas, the shaper of personal destinies, or the impartial judge of behavior. It is merely a piece of software written by random, unthinking, evolutionary processes, class consciousness, sexual yearnings, parental abuse, environmental conditioning, genetic programming, and other deterministic influences prior to the individual or beyond his control.

Is it not ironic that the type of freedom Marcus thought unachievable, political freedom, we now regard as the only freedom possible, while the freedom of mind that Marcus prized so highly now seems unattainable? In the world after Darwin, Marx, and Freud, Marcus forces us to re-examine our concept of freedom and to ask ourselves how much political freedoms are worth if we are the slaves of false opinion and harmful desire. Are we really free in our doing if we are not free in our thinking?

Philosophy as Religion

Marcus' contemporaries identified him as a Stoic philosopher. More needs to be said about this. One of the reasons it is difficult to imagine Marcus' world or to translate his notes into English is that our words, even words like "philosophy," which translates directly from the Greek *philosophia,* often mean vastly different things. Nowadays, we think of philosophy as an academic discipline with many branches, none of which does much to inform everyday life or to demand from its students a particular way of life. Modern philosophy involves endless disputations and offers few if any conclusions, and science has largely superseded it as a source for answers about the nature of the physical universe and human society.

None of this was true of philosophy in the ancient world. Marcus' world abounded in philosophical "schools." On a visit to Athens, he endowed chairs in the four major schools of his time: the Academics (who followed Plato), the Peripatetics (who followed Aristotle), the Epicureans, and the Stoics. All of these schools taught a way of life based on their idiosyncratic knowledge of the nature of the universe. It is true that long before Aristophanes, philosophers were ridiculed for having their heads in the clouds, but even Socrates, one of those to bear the brunt of this joke, never doubted the power of philosophy to teach men how to live and govern well, manage their businesses, and lead their armies.

Ancient philosophers brought everything into their philosophy—whether physics, rhetoric, or ethics—and they sought to find a reasonable place for it in a well-ordered universe. They did not distinguish, as we would today, between the natural and supernatural, the philosophical and theological, gods and rocks, oracles and trees.

> When men hate or blame you, or say hurtful things about you, look deeply into their hearts and see what kind of men they are. You'll see how unnecessary it is to strain after their good opinion. Yet you must still think kindly of them. They are your neighbors. The gods help them as they do you, by dreams and oracles, to win their hearts' desires. (IX.27)

Their interests were both universal and practical. They promised to derive prescriptions for human happiness from what we today would call a scientific understanding of the universe. Adherents to the various philosophical schools, such as Marcus was to Stoicism, were known as "converts," a term the early Christians borrowed to describe themselves in much the same way as they described their religion as a philosophy. To life's most urgent questions, these converts would turn, as Marcus did, to their philosophy:

> What then can guide us through this life? Philosophy, only philosophy. It preserves the inner spirit, keeping it free from blemish

and abuse, master of all pleasures and pains, and prevents it from acting without a purpose or with the intention to deceive, ensuring that we lack nothing, whatever others may do or not do. It accepts the accidents of fate as flowing from the same source as we ourselves, and above all, it waits for death contentedly, viewing it as nothing more than the natural dispersal of those elements composing every living thing. (II.17)

Why practice philosophy? All ancient philosophers, whatever their school, answered this question in the same way. They all claimed to teach how to live the good life and thereby achieve personal happiness. The Stoics placed special emphasis on the mind and the community, or as they often called it, the city. For them, the good life begins in the mind, but one cannot realize the good life cut off from a good society. This accounts for the remarkable balance and creative tension in Marcus between the public and the private man, the man whose thoughts are drawn from his life in society while being given final expression by his free and independent mind. Much of *The Emperor's Handbook* describes this subtle and complex interplay between the mind and the community.

The Stoicism in which Marcus believed is rooted in an all-encompassing nature. Everything in man and in the universe, everything that is or ought to be, everything fated and everything free, and the *logos* or rational principle that informs everything and ties everything together and is ultimately identified with the deity—all of this is found in nature, and there is nothing else. All of this is in a constant state of change. It will end someday in fire, and after that it will be reborn. But meanwhile, it all goes on changing in a recurring pattern and in obedience to universal laws.

Marcus is so tolerant of other philosophical beliefs that some have questioned his Stoic credentials, but this probably demonstrates a misunderstanding either of Marcus' intent or of the nature of philosophical debate during his time. Stoic thinkers borrowed heavily from Plato and from pre-Socratic philosophers like Heraclitus, and many of their teachings were consistent with those of other schools. Even when their teachings differed, Marcus, always a practical man, liked to point out when the effects of their teachings were the same:

Up and down, from age to age, the world's repeating cycles are the same. Either the cosmic mind initiates everything individually (in which case welcome whatever it initiates), or else it initiated things once for all time and every subsequent effect serves also as a cause. Destiny or atoms, what does it matter? If God is discharging every detail, then all is well; and if everything's a matter of chance, still you don't have to be ruled by chance. (IX.28)

It is natural to ask why this tolerance did not extend to Christians, who suffered terrible martyrdoms, especially in Gaul, during the rule of Marcus. Marcus probably knew very little about what Christians believed and may have accepted the popular charges against them of incest and cannibalism. Their refusal to recognize the divinity of the emperor surely made them appear unpatriotic. From the one reference to Christians in his notes, it appears that Marcus viewed them as fanatics with a mad sort of death wish, perhaps as people whose hatred for this life bordered on ingratitude to God, and who in any case shed too many tears at their public executions. They failed to die like Stoics.

> How lovely the soul that is prepared—when its hour comes to slough off this flesh—for extinction, dispersion, or survival! But this readiness should result from a personal decision, not from sheer contrariness like the Christians, and manifest itself deliberately and soberly, in a convincing manner, without histrionics. (XI.3)

This seems a harsh judgment indeed on simple people who were roasted in iron chairs and mauled by wild beasts largely for what they thought rather than for anything they did. Perhaps Marcus, who repeatedly fought off the temptation to end his own long-suffering life prematurely, resented the way these Christians were allowed to end theirs. If so, what a bitter irony for the Christians!

Or perhaps Marcus sensed that this was a movement playing outside the rules of ancient philosophy, one that threatened to undermine the very mind of Rome. Whatever the case, a century later St. Augustine would borrow heavily from the Stoics in creating his brilliant synthesis of the new Christian philosophy, just as St. John had already done by appropriating the Stoic use of *logos* to describe Christ at the beginning of his Gospel. But these Christians identified the *logos* with a Hebrew God who existed before and outside nature, not with a Stoic God synonymous with the universe. This concept of God and the doctrine of the Fall of nature and man changed dramatically the conclusions of ancient philosophy. How could men and women any longer have confidence in answers offered by a reason tainted and a nature corrupted by sin?

Reading *The Emperor's Handbook* should be a liberating experience. It challenges the concepts and categories that frame our modern view of the world and ourselves without our knowing it. It forces us to see the unity in many things our culture places in opposition to one another. The active man and the reflective man, for example; the public and the private; those who wield great power and at the same time think deeply and struggle to make ethical decisions and lead moral lives; those who explore profound truths yet speak and write simply and clearly; those whose passion for substance is as warm as their concern for style; those who value the *freedom to* think independently and wisely as much as the *freedom from* political tyranny. How often do we think of these characteristics belonging together? Yet in Marcus they appear seamlessly united. Even reason and nature, which the Christians declared unreliable and the fiery Romantics later divorced, enjoy a happy if somewhat dull marriage in Marcus.

A Word About Our Translation

Our translation is the result of an exchange of email over a period of four years while we were working as headmasters in France and the United States. A typical exchange involved two to three pages of text, anywhere from one to ten "thoughts." Scot produced a literal translation of Marcus' Greek, which David worked into clear expression of thought with a contemporary American voice. We consulted other translations in English and French to ensure that we were not overlooking a superior interpretation or turn of phrase. The result was then rechecked against the original Greek.

Marcus makes frequent use of words that Greek readers recognize as being part of the technical vocabulary of Stoicism. In this sense Marcus' decision to write in Greek is as obvious as the choice of an eighteenth-century military engineer to write in French or of a twenty-first-century marketing executive to write in English. Once translated out of Greek, these terms lose their precise connotation and well-defined associations. We decided early on to avoid any attempt at a systematic translation of these terms. We sought instead to render the meaning of each as clearly and completely as possible, considering the context in which it was used and the best equivalent in modern American usage, and we did not avoid paraphrase if that seemed the best way to capture Marcus' meaning.

Fortunately, there are excellent references available for those who want to explore the nuances and intricacies of Stoic philosophy and the meaning of its technical jargon. A good place to begin is Jacques Brunschwig's article on Stoicism in *Le Savoir Grec, dictionnaire critique* (Paris: Flammarion, 1996), in English translation as *Greek Thought: A Guide to Classical Knowledge* (Cambridge, Mass.: Harvard University Press Reference Library, 2000). Another French scholar, Pierre Hadot, offers a compelling and comprehensive interpretation of Marcus' thought in his book *La Citadelle intérieure* (Paris: Librairie Arthème Fayard, 1992), now also in English, as *The Inner Citadel* (Cambridge, Mass.: Harvard University Press, 1998). Finally, R. B. Rutherford's *The Meditations of Marcus Aurelius: A Study* (Oxford, England: Oxford University Press, 1988) restores Marcus' book as a literary as well as a philosophical and devotional classic.

We wish to acknowledge the debt of gratitude we owe to the friends who encouraged us with this project, including George Zimmar, Guy Monnot, and Tracy Simmons. We are grateful to the scholars and former teachers whose helpful comments and good opinion of our work corrected our more egregious errors and shored up our confidence, in particular, Scot's professor of Greek at Dartmouth, William C. Scott, his former pupil and assistant professor of classics at Oberlin College, Benjamin Todd Lee, and David's philosophy tutor at Oxford, David A. Rees, who also wrote the introduction to the 1960 edition of Everyman's Farquharson translation. We deeply appreciate the enthusiasm of Bill Westbrook, former president and creative director of Fallon McElligott, and his colleagues Tom Hale and Kerry Feuerman. These men recognized in our translation Marcus' appeal to a much wider contemporary audience than scholars, and they challenged us to think through the design and marketing implications of this appeal. And finally, we thank our wives, Marie and Mary Elizabeth, for their patience, wisdom, and loving support.

Our work habits, daily concerns, and brotherhood allowed us to imagine a certain sympathy with the probable practice of the second-century philosopher-emperor-general. An hour or two of written thought exercise, stolen at the end of a day of managing people, fulfilling social and religious obligations, and being husband, father, and citizen, can revive the spirits. The refreshing candor with which Marcus voices his daily frustrations and the vigor with which he admonishes himself won our hearts and inspired us to bear our much lighter burdens with less complaint and far more gratitude.

DVH/CSH

BOOK ONE

1 · I am indebted to my grandfather Verus for his good disposition and sweet temper.

2 · From my father's reputation and my memory of him, I learned modesty and manliness.

3 · From my mother I learned to fear God and to be generous, to refuse not only to do evil but to think it, and a simplicity of life far removed from the habits of the rich.

4 · Thanks to my great-grandfather, I didn't have to waste my time in the public schools but had good tutors at home instead and learned that one cannot spend too much money on such things.

5 · My tutor taught me not to take sides in circus contests (Green or Blue, Light-Shield or Heavy), to love hard work, to limit my desires, to rely on myself, to keep my nose out of other people's affairs, and to turn a deaf ear to gossip.

6 · From Diognetus I learned to shun trivialities; to doubt the claims of wonder-workers and wizards about spells and exorcisms; to refrain from cock-fighting and other forms of gambling; to hear criticism without taking offense; to acquire a taste for philosophy—first for Baccheius, then for Tandasis and Marcianus; to write serious essays while just a boy; and to prefer a hard bed of planks covered with a pelt, and all the other rigors of a Greek upbringing.

7 · Rusticus made me realize that my life needed correction, my character training. He kept me from making a fool of myself by trying to impress others with clever sophistries, obscure speculations,

and lofty exhortations, or by posing as a man above temptation or as the great lover of mankind.

He taught me

- to rid my speech of rhetorical devices and poetical flourishes and fancy conceits;
- not to walk around the house in lavish dress and to avoid other affectations of this sort;
- to write simple letters like the one he wrote my mother from Sinuessa;
- to be quick to accept the apology of anyone who has hurt or offended me;
- to read books for detailed understanding and not to settle for general summaries or accept uncritically the opinions of reviewers.

He also introduced me to the Discourses of Epictetus, which he lent me from his personal library.

8 · Apollonius taught me to take matters into my own hands and not to temporize, not to leave them to chance, and not—not for one instant—to let reason out of my sight. From him I acquired the habit of unshakable composure, even in the midst of acute pain, or at the death of a child, or during a prolonged illness. He was living proof that it is possible to marry passionate endeavor to a gentle disposition, for he intently untangled the skein of ideas with inexhaustible patience. Yet he obviously considered his practical experience and his pedagogical skill as the least of his gifts. Moreover, he showed me how to accept the apparent tributes and favors of friends without either feeling myself under obligation or feigning indifference.

9 · Generosity of spirit I learned from Sextus. He offered a fine example of the father who governs his family well and of a life lived in conformity with nature, of high-mindedness without pomposity, of genuine concern for friends, and of patience with fools and with those whose opinions have no basis in fact. He tuned his lyre

so perfectly to those around him that they took more delight in his company than in any flattery, all the while holding him in highest esteem.

I also admired his ability to discover and organize, in an insightful and systematic way, the rules for living a good life, as well as his ability to suppress all signs of anger or any other emotion while at the same time displaying great human affection. He demonstrated how to praise without overdoing it and how to possess knowledge without showing off.

> HE DEMONSTRATED
> HOW TO PRAISE WITHOUT
> OVERDOING IT AND HOW
> TO POSSESS KNOWLEDGE
> WITHOUT SHOWING OFF.

10 ▸ Alexander the professor of rhetoric warned me against gratuitous fault finding. Rather than point out in humiliating fashion some mispronunciation, lapse in grammar, or flaw in diction, it is better to introduce the correct word or phrase tactfully in a response. Do this while expressing agreement with what has been said, or while asking for more discussion of the topic.

11 ▸ Fronto helped me to see how privilege and power breed malice, deceit, and hypocrisy and how often those whom we call "Patricians" lack natural human feeling.

12 ▸ Alexander the Platonist cautioned me against saying or writing in a letter, either too often or without absolutely needing to, "I'm too busy," as well as against using the demands of work as a constant excuse for ducking my social obligations and familial duties.

13 ▸ Catulus taught me not to ignore a friend who is cross with me, even if I have done nothing to deserve his bad temper, but to seek to regain his affection. He taught me to be generous in praising my teachers, as we see in the memoirs of Domitius and Athenodotus, and to be genuine in loving my children.

14 · To my brother Severus I owe my love of family, truth, and justice; my introduction to Thraseas, Helvidius, Cato, and Brutus; and the idea of a state in which all men are equal under the law and free to say what they think, and of an empire that respects above all else the liberty of its subjects. He exhibited a measured and steadfast regard for philosophy, an inclination to help others, an enthusiasm for good works, optimism, and confidence in the love of his friends. Those of whom he disapproved never had cause to wonder why, and his friends never had to guess at what was on his mind—so honest and outspoken a man was he.

15 · Maximus set an example of self-mastery, steadiness of purpose, and good cheer that no circumstance, not even illness, could extinguish. He combined in beautiful measure gravity with charm, and he did whatever needed to be done without making a fuss. Everyone believed that what he said was what he thought and that he never acted with an intention to do harm or give offense. Nothing surprised or frightened him, and he never seemed to be in a hurry or slow to accomplish a task. He was neither intimidated and embarrassed on the one hand, nor aggressive and suspicious on the other. So giving, forgiving, and loyal was he by nature that he appeared to be a man whose virtues were inborn rather than acquired. It is unimaginable that anyone ever felt inferior or superior around him, perhaps as a result of his pleasing sense of humor.

16 · From my (adoptive) father, I learned

- courtesy and unswerving loyalty to decisions taken after hard thought;
- indifference to pomp and praise;
- industry and steadiness;
- a keen interest in any proposal for the public good;
- reward given strictly to merit;
- the knowledge of when to press on and when to ease up;
- chaste habits and the love of companionship.

My father allowed his friends the freedom to eat and travel with him as they pleased, and he took no offense when their own affairs detained them. In business meetings, he never accepted a first impression or a plausible answer without subjecting it to detailed and searching inquiry. Smiling and calm, he kept his own counsel and did not make capricious or extravagant demands on his friends. In all things great and small, he exercised foresight and prepared down to the last detail for every eventuality, yet without making a big production of it.

My father taught me

- to refuse public applause and to eschew all forms of flattery;
- to be vigilant in managing the affairs of the empire, to be frugal in spending from the public purse, and to put up with the inevitable grumbling that will follow from those who want something for nothing;
- to avoid being superstitious toward the gods and obsequious toward men, knowing that it is better to be sober and self-reliant and to distrust the novelty of invention and the vulgarity of popular esteem.

My father enjoyed, without pretention or self-indulgence, the luxuries that his fortune lavished upon him; but when these were not available, he never seemed to miss them. No one ever mistook him for a pundit, a toady, or a pedant, nor failed to recognize in him the qualities of a mature and accomplished man insensible to flattery and able to govern himself as well as others. He respected sound learning and those who seek the truth, and he remained on good terms with the rest, but from a distance.

From my father, I learned

- a cheerful and friendly disposition, within reason;
- prudent care for the body—which he neither abused in luxurious living, nor pampered with excessive exercise and diet, nor neglected unduly, and thereby kept himself almost free from doctors, medicines, and salves;
- a true regard for those who have mastered a particular skill or subject—the art of public speaking, for example, or a knowledge of law or history or any other subject—

and a genuine desire to see that each of these receives the honor due him.

A true Roman, my father didn't worry about keeping up appearances. He felt no anxiety or stress. He took pleasure in treating familiar subjects repeatedly and in staying in the same old places. Even after the most violent headaches, he would return quickly and energetically to his work. He hated secrets and kept them only when affairs of state demanded it. Moderation and good taste marked his celebration of holidays, his public works, his distribution of relief to the poor, and his other official acts. Whatever he did he did out of a sense of duty to meet a real need, not to gain popularity.

My father never bathed at odd hours or got carried away with his building projects. Never did he pretend to be a connoisseur of food and wine, a fashion expert, or an authority on good looks. His clothing, generally of Lanuvian wool, was made in Lorium, where he had a country house. Indeed, the way my father treated the tax collector of Tusculum, who hounded him by mistake, is a good example of his manner. No black looks, no harsh words, no aggressive behavior that can lead others to say, "He's got a mean streak." None of this. Instead, a measured and rational assessment of everything, without haste or hesitation, rendering judgments so calm, fitting, forceful, logical, and harmonious that one could say of him what was once said of Socrates: that he could either enjoy or abstain from those things whose enjoyment weakens and whose abstinence strengthens most men.

These things I learned from my father: strength, steadfastness, and moderation on all occasions, a spirit perfectly balanced and indomitable, like the one he showed during the illness which took him away.

17 · I have the gods to thank for good grandparents, good parents, a good sister, good teachers, good companions, relatives, and friends—almost all of them good. I also thank the gods for keeping me from abusing any of them, although I possess a character that might easily have allowed me to do so had the goodness of the gods not spared me from circumstances that would have put me to the test.

Thanks to the gods I didn't spend much time while growing up with my grandfather's mistress and preserved the flower of my youth, waiting for the proper time to demonstrate my virility, even putting it off a bit.

The gods gave me a father who ruled over me and rid me of any trace of arrogance and showed me that one can live in a palace without bodyguards, extravagant attire, chandeliers, statues, and other luxuries. He taught me that it is possible to live instead pretty much in the manner of a private citizen without losing any of the dignity and authority a ruler must possess to discharge his imperial duties effectively.

The gods provided me with a brother whose character inspired me to look after my own and whose respect and affection all the while disarmed me.

I thank the gods for children without mental or physical handicaps.

I bless the gods for not letting my education in rhetoric, poetry, and other literary studies come easily to me, and thereby sparing me from an absorbing interest in these subjects. I am thankful that I wasted no time in appointing my teachers to the positions they seemed to aspire to and did not put them off on the pretext that they were too young, promising that I would shower them with honors later on. I am thankful too that I came to know Apollonius, Rusticus, and Maximus.

The gods have provided me with clear and compelling signs of what it means to live in conformity to nature. They did their part. So far as their gifts, aid, and inspiration are concerned, nothing prevented me from following the path prescribed by nature. If from time to time I have strayed from this path, the fault lies with me and with my failure to heed the gods' signs, or rather, their explicit instructions.

I must have the gods to thank for these:

- the fact that my body has stood up so long under the strain of the life I lead;
- for never having touched Benedicta or Theodotus and for having recovered gracefully from my later infatuations;

- › for not having done anything I would later regret during one of my frequent fallings-out with Rusticus;
- › and for allowing my mother, who was fated to die young, to spend her last years with me.

Thanks to the gods, whenever I felt like helping somebody in need, I was never told that I lacked sufficient funds, nor was I ever in the position of needing to look to somebody else for help.

I must also thank the gods for a wife like mine—so sweet, so affectionate, so unassuming—and for an unending supply of excellent teachers for my children.

Specifically, I am in the gods' debt for the dreams that cured me from coughing up blood and from vertigo and for the guidance of the oracle at Caieta, "It's up to you!"

I thank the gods that when I became interested in philosophy I did not fall into the hands of a sophist, or throw away my time reading fictive histories, sifting through obscure arguments, or gazing at the stars.

> "IT'S UP TO YOU!"

All these good things came "from the hand of God and with the help of Fortune."

BOOK TWO

Written Among the Quadi on the River Gran

1 ’ First thing every morning tell yourself: today I am going to meet a busybody, an ingrate, a bully, a liar, a schemer, and a boor. Ignorance of good and evil has made them what they are. But I know that the good is by nature beautiful and the bad ugly, and I know that these wrong-doers are by nature my brothers, not by blood or breeding, but by being similarly endowed with reason and sharing in the divine. None of them can harm me, for none can force me to do wrong against my will, and I cannot be angry with a brother or resent him, for we were born into this world to work together like the feet, hands, eyelids, and upper and lower rows of teeth. To work against one another is contrary to nature, and what could be more like working against someone than resenting or abandoning him?

2 ’ What am I but a little flesh, a little breath, and the thinking part that rules the whole? Forget your books! They aren't any part of you. And as someone who is dying, you should disregard the flesh as well: it is nothing but blood and bones and a network of muscle tissues, nerves, and arteries. Breath! What is that? A puff of wind that is never the same, being sucked in one moment and blown out the next. That leaves the thinking part, the part meant to rule. Now that you are old, it is time you stopped allowing it to be enslaved, jerked about by every selfish whim, grumbling at its present lot one moment and bemoaning the future the next.

3 ’ The gods sustain and guide all their works. Not even the vicissitudes of fortune are contrary to nature or to the providential ordering of the universe. It all flows from the gods, who determine what is needed for the welfare of the whole universe, of which you are a part.

27

What is good for each part of nature like yourself is whatever the whole of nature provides and whatever tends to sustain it. Now it is change that sustains the whole universe—both the simple changes occurring within individual parts as well as the complex changes occurring among parts in combination. Let these thoughts set your mind at ease, and keep them as your guiding principles. Thirst no more for books, so that you will not die mumbling to yourself, but at peace, truly, and with your heart full of thanksgiving to the gods.

4 · Remember how long you have procrastinated, and how consistently you have failed to put to good use your suspended sentence from the gods. It is about time you realized the nature of the universe (of which you are a part) and of the power that rules it (to which your part owes its existence). Your days are numbered. Use them to throw open the windows of your soul to the sun. If you do not, the sun will soon set, and you with it.

5 · Every hour be firmly resolved, as becomes a Roman and a man, to accomplish the work at hand with fitting and unaffected dignity, goodwill, freedom, and justice. Banish from your thoughts all other considerations. This is possible if you perform each act as if it were your last, rejecting every frivolous distraction, every denial of the rule of reason, every pretentious gesture, vain show, and whining complaint against the decrees of fate. Do you see what little is required of a man to live a well-tempered and god-fearing life? Obey these precepts, and the gods will ask nothing more.

6 · Go on abusing yourself, O my soul! Not long and you will lose the opportunity to show yourself any respect. We have only one life to live, and yours is almost over. Because you have chosen not to respect yourself, you have made your happiness subject to the opinions others have of you.

> BECAUSE YOU HAVE CHOSEN
> NOT TO RESPECT YOURSELF,
> YOU HAVE MADE YOUR HAPPINESS
> SUBJECT TO THE OPINIONS
> OTHERS HAVE OF YOU.

7 · Does the news bother you? Do you worry about things out of your control? Then take the time to concentrate your mind in the acquisition of some new and useful knowledge and stop it from flitting about. By the same token, guard against making the mistake of those who keep themselves so busy trying to gain control that they wear themselves out and lose their sense of direction, having no purpose to guide their actions or even their thoughts.

8 · Not knowing what other people are thinking is not the cause of much human misery, but failing to understand the workings of one's own mind is bound to lead to unhappiness.

9 · Be mindful at all times of the following: the nature of the whole universe, the nature of the part that is me, the relation of the one to the other, the one so vast, the other so small. No one can ever prevent me from saying and doing what is in complete conformity with the whole of which I am so small yet integral a part.

10 · When making a not uncommon comparison between faults of character, the philosopher Theophrastus claims that sins of desire are worse than sins of anger. Whereas the angry man seems to reject reason painfully and with a certain unconscious contraction of the spirit, he who sins out of desire, desperate for pleasure, appears more self-seeking and womanish. He was right and worthy of his philosophy to censure sins undertaken for pleasure more heartily than those accompanied by pain. In general, the one is more like a victim fired to anger first by the pain of an injustice and then by the pain of his response, while the other deliberately desires what he knows to be wrong in the hope of deriving pleasure from it.

11 · Act, speak, and think like a man ready to depart this life in the next breath. If there are gods, you have no reason to fear your flight from the land of the living, for they will not let any harm come to you; and if there are no gods, or they are indifferent to the affairs of men, why wish to go on living in a world without them or without their guidance and care? But in fact, there are gods, and they do care

about men, and they have made it possible for men to guard themselves against what is truly evil. Were there any evil in what awaits us, they would have given us the means of avoiding it.

Besides, how can a man's life be made worse by what does not make him morally worse? Nature cannot possibly have overlooked such an obvious contradiction out of ignorance, or having been aware of it, failed to protect us from it or to resolve it. Nor can nature have erred so egregiously, through want of power or skill, in allowing so-called goods and evils to rain down indiscriminately on good and bad men in roughly equal measure. The truth is this: since death and life, glory and shame, pain and pleasure, wealth and poverty, all of these happen to the good and bad alike, without making the one worse or the other better, none of these things can be in itself either good or bad.

12 ، How swiftly everything disappears—bodies in space and the memory of them in time! So it is with anything that touches our senses, especially those that entice us with the promise of pleasure, or terrify us with the threat of pain, or puff us up with pride and self-importance. The mind readily grasps how worthless and contemptible, filthy, fleeting, and moribund these things are. It makes an accurate appraisal of those whose opinions and voices confer fame, and it apprehends what it means to die. Considered by itself, stripped by reason of all the superstitions surrounding it, death is just another work of nature—and only a small child fears works of nature. In fact, death is not just one of nature's works, it is also of essential benefit to her.

Observe how man touches the divine and with what part of his being this contact is made and how that part is then affected.

13 ، Nothing is more pathetic than feverishly circling the earth and "probing into its depths," as Pindar puts it, to guess what other people are thinking, while all the time failing to realize that one only needs to attend to the inner spirit and to serve it with unswerving devotion. What is this service? To preserve the spirit from passion, from aimlessness, and from resenting what comes from gods and men. We revere the work of the gods because it is excellent, and we

love the work of men because hearts and hands like our own have fashioned it, even if at times this work arouses pity owing to man's ignorance of good and evil, a blindness no less profound than the inability to distinguish black from white.

14 › Were you to live three thousand years, or even thirty thousand, remember that a man can lose only the life he is living, and he can live no other life than the one he loses. Whether he lives a long time or a short time amounts to the same thing, for the present moment is of equal duration for everyone, and that is all any man possesses. This is why the loss of life seems so momentary. A man cannot lose the past or the future—how can he be robbed of what is not his? Remember, then, these two truths: first, that everything from the beginning is just the same pattern repeating itself, and it makes no difference whether you watch this same show for a hundred years, or for two hundred, or for all eternity; and second, that the man who dies young loses not a jot more than the man who dies old. A man can only be deprived of the present moment, for this is all he has, and how can a man lose what he doesn't possess?

15 › "Our assumptions determine everything." The problem with these words attributed to Monimus the Cynic is plain enough, but if we consider them in the context of larger truths, they reveal an important insight.

16 › A man's soul abuses itself in a number of ways, first and foremost by becoming, as much as it can, a cancerous growth, a foreign body in the universe. Complaining against the nature of things is a revolt against nature, which is made up of all the natures of its many parts. Second, it does violence to itself when it scorns another man, or seeks to do him harm out of anger. Third, it wrongs itself when it yields to pleasure or pain. Fourth, when it wears a mask, and speaks or acts falsely or insincerely. Fifth, whenever its actions and efforts have no apparent purpose and cause it to operate at random and without consequence, for even the slightest act should have some end in mind. The end for all rational beings is to obey the reason and law of the one hallowed City and Republic.

17 ˒ What is man? His life a point in time, his substance a watery fluxion, his perceptions dim, his flesh food for worms, his soul a vortex, his destiny inscrutable, his fame doubtful. In sum, the things of the flesh are a river, the things of the soul all dream and smoke; life is war and a posting abroad; posthumous fame ends in oblivion.

What then can guide us through this life? Philosophy, only philosophy. It preserves the inner spirit, keeping it free from blemish and abuse, master of all pleasures and pains, and prevents it from acting without a purpose or with the intention to deceive, ensuring that we lack nothing, whatever others may do or not do. It accepts the accidents of fate as flowing from the same source as we ourselves, and above all, it waits for death contentedly, viewing it as nothing more than the natural dispersal of those elements composing every living thing. If the constant transformation of one element into another is in no way dreadful, why should we fear the sudden dispersal and transformation of all our bodily elements? This conforms with nature, and nothing natural is bad.

BOOK THREE

Written at Carnuntum (now Hainburg, Austria).

1 · It is not enough to watch the days we've already lived pile up on one side and those that remain melt away on the other. We must also consider that even if we were to live longer, it is not at all certain our minds would retain their ability to understand what is happening around us or to grasp its significance, whether human or divine. Just because the mind begins to go doesn't mean that breathing and eating are impaired, or that imagination, desire, and the like are inhibited. But without a mind, man is no longer able to be the master of himself, to understand exactly what is expected of him, to judge the evidence of his senses, to know when it's time to quit this life, or in other words, to make any of those calculations that require an intellect in reasonably good working order. We must get on with our lives, then, not only because we are closing on death with each passing day, but because our mental capacities may desert us before death decides to take us.

2 · We should also pause to consider how charming and graceful are the unexpected effects of nature's work. When bread is baking, for example, cracks appear in the crust. Although these would seem to confound the baker's design, they attract our attention and help to arouse our appetite. Figs too burst open just when they are best to eat, and olives left on the tree to rot achieve a most exquisite beauty. Similarly, the golden grain's drooping head, the lion's furrowed brow, the boar's foaming snout, and so many other details, if taken out of context, are not all that attractive, but when seen in their natural setting, they complete a picture and please the eye.

In this way, the perceptive man, profoundly curious about the workings of nature, will take a peculiar pleasure in everything, even in the humble or ungainly parts that contribute to the making of the whole. The actual jaws of living beasts will delight him as much as their representations by artists and sculptors. With a discerning eye, he will warm to an old man's strength or an old woman's beauty while admiring with cool detachment the seductive charms of youth. The world is full of wonders like these that will appeal only to those who study nature closely and develop a real affinity for her works.

3 · After curing many illnesses, Hippocrates became ill himself and died. The Chaldaean astrologers predicted the deaths of many before their own fatal hours struck. Alexander, Pompey, and Julius Caesar sacked and ruined countless cities and maimed and slaughtered untold thousands of soldiers and horses, and then they too departed this life. Heraclitus, after endless speculation on the destruction of the universe by fire, drowned in his own juices, plastered with cowdung. Lice got the better of Democritus, and vermin of another sort killed Socrates.

So what's the point of it all? Simply this. You embarked; you sailed; you landed. Now, disembark! If it is to start a new life, you will find the gods there too. If it is to lose all consciousness, you will be liberated from the tyranny of pleasure and pain and from your bondage to an earthly shell that is vastly inferior to the master contained in it. For the spirit is intelligent and godlike whereas the body is blood and dust.

4 · Do not waste the rest of your life speculating about others in ways that are not to your mutual advantage. Think of all that might be accomplished in the time you throw away—distracted from the voice of your own true and reasonable self—wondering what the next man is up to and why, what he's saying, or thinking, or plotting.

Purge your mind of all aimless and idle thoughts, especially those that pry into the affairs of others or wish them ill. Get in the habit of limiting yourself only to those thoughts that—if you are suddenly asked, "What are you thinking at this moment?"—enable you to reply without equivocation or hesitation, "This" or "That." In this way, you show the world a simple and kindly man, a good neighbor, someone who is indifferent to sensual pleasures and luxuries and untouched by jealousy, envy, mistrust, or any other thought you would blush to admit.

This sort of man, determined to be counted among the best in the pursuit of virtue, is a veritable priest and minister of the gods, especially of the god that dwells within him and keeps him untainted by pleasure, unharmed by pain, safe from any wrong, innocent of all evil, a mighty warrior in the greatest warfare of all—the struggle against passion's dominion. With justice like marrow in his bones, he delights from the depths of his being in whatever happens, in whatever fate the gods allow. He never—except to achieve some great good on behalf of others—worries about what someone else might be saying, doing, or thinking. He minds his own business and keeps his gaze fixed on the pattern of his own destiny, making sure that he performs his work well and believing that his fate is good since it is subject to the universal good.

He remembers his kinship with all rational beings and never abandons his natural inclination to care for others, but he listens only to the opinions of those who live in conscious accord with nature. As for those who do not live in this way, he observes how they live and what sort of vile company they keep, day and night, at home and abroad. He attaches no importance whatsoever to the praise of these men, who can find no reason to praise themselves.

> PURGE YOUR MIND OF ALL
> AIMLESS AND IDLE THOUGHTS,
> ESPECIALLY THOSE THAT PRY
> INTO THE AFFAIRS OF OTHERS
> OR WISH THEM ILL.

5 · Do not act unwillingly, or selfishly, or impulsively, or tentatively. Do not dress your thought in much fine talk. Be short in speech and restrained in action. Let the god who dwells within you command a manly man, a seasoned veteran, a statesman, a Roman, a leader who stands ready to give up his life when the retreat is sounded, without requiring an oath or looking around for witnesses. Show by a cheerful look that you don't need the help or comfort of others. Standing up—not propped up.

6 ˒ If life offers you anything better than justice, truth, wisdom, and courage—or in other words, better than the peace that comes from acting in accord with reason or in accord with destiny when events are outside your control—if, as I was saying, life offers you anything better than this, embrace it with your whole heart and enjoy it to the full.

But if life offers you nothing better than your indwelling spirit—the same spirit that governs your emotions, guides your thoughts, "tears you away," as Socrates used to say, "from the titillation of the senses," obeys the gods, and serves mankind—if by comparison with this spirit you find everything else trifling and base, then give not the slightest foothold to anything else. Nothing will sooner prevent your true spirit from flourishing or be more difficult to root out than the distraction of a divided loyalty.

Nothing whatsoever—neither popularity, nor wealth, nor power, nor the pleasures of the flesh, nor anything of the sort—should compete in your affection for the good that flows from reason and neighborliness. Although for awhile these inferior loves may seem quite compatible with an orderly life, they will soon overpower and destroy you. Simply and freely choose what is best, and never let go of it.

"But the best is whatever works to my advantage," you say.

Then study your advantage carefully. If it's to the advantage of your reasonable self, seize hold of it. If it's merely to the advantage of your animal self, admit it and don't try to pretend it's more than that. Only be sure of your judgment.

7 ˒ There is no present advantage in anything that may someday force you to break your word, or to lose respect for yourself, or to hate, suspect, or curse another, or to pretend to be other than what you are, or to lust after what you'd be ashamed to seek openly. The man who gives pride of place to reason and to his indwelling spirit—and remains the devoted servant of each—plays no parts, utters no complaints, and craves neither the wilderness nor the crowd. In fact, he lives without pursuing or fleeing anything at all. Knowing how much longer his soul will travel around in his body—whether for a short time or a long time—is of no interest to him. If the journey

were suddenly to end, he would step out of his frame with the same dignity and simplicity that characterize all his actions. All his life he has cared only about this: to take no detours from the high road of reason and social responsibility.

8 · In the mind of a disciplined and pure man, you will find no sign of infection, no running sores, no wounds that haven't healed. It will not be this man's fate to quit life unfulfilled like the actor who fails to complete his lines and walks offstage before the play is ended. What is more, there is nothing obsequious or conceited about him; he neither depends on others nor is afraid to ask for help; he answers to no man for who he is and for what he does, yet he hides nothing.

9 · Treat with utmost respect your power of forming opinions, for this power alone guards you against making assumptions that are contrary to nature and judgments that overthrow the rule of reason. It enables you to learn from experience, to live in harmony with others, and to walk in the way of the gods.

10 · Tossing aside everything else, hold fast to these few truths. We live only in the present, in this fleet-footed moment. The rest is lost and behind us, or ahead of us and may never be found. Little of life we know, little the plot of earth on which we dwell, little the memory of even the most famous who have lived, and this memory itself is preserved by generations of little men, who know little about themselves and far less about those who died long ago.

> WE LIVE ONLY IN THE PRESENT,
> IN THIS FLEET-FOOTED MOMENT.
> THE REST IS LOST
> AND BEHIND US, OR AHEAD OF US
> AND MAY NEVER BE FOUND.

11 · To these truths add one more: whenever you see or imagine something, make a precise mental picture of it, stripped to its bare essence and divorced from its surroundings; call it by its proper name, and name each of the parts that compose it and into which it will

someday decompose. Nothing produces greatness of mind like the habit of examining methodically and honestly everything we encounter in this life and of determining its place in the order of things, its intended use, its value to the whole universe, and its worth to man in his role as citizen of that world City in which all other cities are but households.

Ask yourself, "What is causing the image or idea now forming in my brain? What elements compose it? How long will it last? What virtue does it require of me—gentleness, for example, or courage, honesty, loyalty, simplicity, self-reliance, and so on?" At each encounter like this you must say, "This comes from God; or this happened by sheer coincidence through some chance combination of circumstance and some random blow of fortune; or this is a man's doing, a brother or a neighbor who doesn't know how to act in accord with his true nature, but since I do possess this knowledge, I will treat him kindly and fairly as the law of my being demands, while bearing in mind that pleasure has no power to weaken or pain to harm me unless I let them."

12 · If you pursue the matter at hand along the straight path of reason, advancing with intensity, vigor, and grace, and without being distracted along the way; if you keep your divine spirit pure and blameless, as though this were the moment to give it back; if expecting nothing and fearing nothing, you are content to act in accord with nature and to speak with heroic honesty—then you will live well. And no power on earth can stop you.

13 · Just as surgeons always keep their scalpels and other instruments handy to provide emergency care on demand, so you should keep your principles with you at all times, ready to delve into anything human or divine, remembering in even the most routine operation how intimately the two are related. Indeed, no human action can be well taken without reference to the divine, nor the reverse.

> NO HUMAN ACTION CAN BE WELL TAKEN WITHOUT REFERENCE TO THE DIVINE

14 ‣ Stop jumping off the track. You don't have time to reread your diaries, or the lives of the ancient Greeks and Romans, or the passages from their writings that you've collected for your old age. Throw off vain hope and sprint to the finish. If you care about yourself at all, come to your own aid while there's still time.

15 ‣ They fail to see all that it means to steal, to plant, to buy, to live in peace, to do what is right. To see all this requires an organ other than the eye.

16 ‣ Body, soul, mind—the body for sensations, the soul for the impulse to act, the mind for guiding principles. Yet even the cattle in the field feel sensations; even wild beasts, perverts, a Phalaris, or a Nero are attached to the puppet strings of impulse; even men who deny the existence of God, betray their country, and engage in shameful practices behind closed doors possess minds to guide them.

Having all this in common with the likes of these, there remains only one distinguishing mark of the good man: his love and delight in the thread of his own destiny and his refusal to soil or upset with an orgy of sensations the divine spirit dwelling within him, where a serene peace reigns and God is obeyed and no untrue words are spoken and no unjust deeds performed. Even if everyone else questions his ability to live so simply, modestly, and happily, he doesn't let their doubts disturb him or divert him from the road leading to his life's destination, which he intends to reach pure and peaceful and prepared to take his leave in unforced allegiance to his fate.

BOOK FOUR

1 · When the sovereign spirit within us is true to nature, it stands poised and ready to adjust to every change in circumstance and to seize each new opportunity. It doesn't approach an object with prejudice or preconception, but handles each thing dispassionately before embracing it and, if necessary, finds advantage in what opposes it. It is like fire in this regard. Whereas a feeble flame might suffocate under a pile of dry sticks, a robust fire consumes everything it touches. The more objects of any kind heaped on it, the higher it rises, the hotter it burns.

2 · Never act without purpose and resolve, or without the means to finish the job.

3 · Everyone dreams of the perfect vacation—in the country, by the sea, or in the mountains. You too long to get away and find that idyllic spot, yet how foolish . . . when at any time you are capable of finding that perfect vacation in yourself. Nowhere is there a more idyllic spot, a vacation home more private and peaceful, than in one's own mind, especially when it is furnished in such a way that the merest inward glance induces ease (and by ease I mean the effects of an orderly and well-appointed mind, neither lavish nor crude). Take this vacation as often as you like, and so charge your spirit. But do not prolong these meditative moments beyond what is necessary to send you back to your work free of anxiety and full of vigor and good cheer.

What makes you anxious anyway? The wrongs of others? Well, consider the following: reasonable men and women are made for one another; patience is a part of justice; and no one willingly does wrong. Think of all those who filled their days with anger, suspicion, hatred, and fighting—and are now dust. Think on them and what has become of their wrongdoing. This ought to calm you down.

Or is it your lot in life that makes you anxious? Then it's time to remind yourself of the need to choose between an all-seeing Providence and blind atoms. Remember too the extent to which the universe is like a well-ordered and well-governed city.

Or are you in some sort of physical pain or distress? Recall that the mind, once it withdraws into itself and becomes aware of its own awesome powers, is no longer lulled or tossed about by the lazy or turbulent currents of the body. In addition, don't forget what your philosophy teaches about pleasure and pain.

Or are you tormented by what others may think of you? Look then on how soon everything is forgotten, and gaze into the abyss of infinite time. Hear the hollowness of the applause, and ponder the fickleness of those who are applauding you while you consider the narrowness of the stage on which you pant after their plaudits. The entire earth is but a piece of dust blowing through the firmament, and the inhabited part of the earth a small fraction thereof. So, in such a grand space, how many do you think will think of you, and what will their thoughts be worth?

Well then, remember to take those little vacations into yourself. Whatever you do, don't be troubled or anxious, but be free, and look at things like a man, a human being, a citizen, a part of the creation that must die. Chief among the thoughts close at hand, keep these two: first, that nothing outside the mind can disturb it—trouble comes from the mind's opinion of what lies outside it; and second, that everything you now see will change in a moment and soon be no more. Can you even begin to count the changes you have already witnessed?

This world is change; this life, opinion.

4 · If the mind is common to us all, then so is reason that enables us to understand and tells us how to treat one another. If this is so, then we hold the law in common as well. We are fellow citizens, subject to one unwritten constitution, and the world is, as it were, a city. Indeed, what other citizenship is shared by the whole human race? From this common city, we derive mind, reason, and law, and if this is not so, where do they then come from? Just as the earthy part of me is taken from the earth, the liquid part from another element, air

from another source, and the hot and fiery part from yet another—for nothing comes from nothing or returns to nothing—so my mind must come from somewhere.

5 ʾ Death, like birth, is one of nature's mysteries, the combining of primal elements and dissolving of the same into the same. Nothing about death should shame or upset us, for it is entirely in keeping with our nature as rational animals and with the law governing us.

6 ʾ What do you expect from people like him? Certain effects naturally and necessarily flow from certain causes. To want him to behave otherwise is like asking the sap not to flow in a fig tree. Besides, what's the point of fretting about it? In a moment, you will both be dead, and a moment later, no one will even be able to remember your names.

7 ʾ Stop trying to make something of it, and you will rid yourself of the notion, "I've been wronged." Overcome your hurt feelings or injured pride in this way, and you will get rid of the wrong itself.

8 ʾ What doesn't make a man worse cannot make his life any worse, nor can it harm him either from within or without.

9 ʾ Nature insists upon whatever benefits the whole.

10 ʾ "Whatever happens happens justly." Pay close attention and you will see that this is so. By this I don't mean only that justice will result from whatever happens, but I mean that a just process will also be served, as is the case when payment is made for work or prizes are awarded for victory. So be particularly scrupulous in this and continue as you have begun, a decent man performing every deed conscious of the most rigorous requirements of goodness. Preserve this sense in every act.

11 ʾ Don't look at the world through the eyes of an insolent and unhappy man, or judge things as he would; but see life as it truly is.

12 ' Arm yourself for action with these two thoughts: first, do only what your sovereign and lawgiving reason tells you is for the good of others; and second, do not hesitate to change course if someone is able to show you where you are mistaken or point out a better way. But be persuaded only by arguments based on justice and the common good, never by what appeals to your taste for pleasure or popularity.

13 ' Do you possess reason? "Yes." Then why not use it? Once reason goes to work for you, what more can you need?

14 ' You are but a part sustained by the whole. Someday your part will be reclaimed by what formed it, or rather, through a process of change you will re-enter the womb of reason from which you were born.

15 ' Many grains of incense will fall upon the same altar. One drops early, another late—it makes no difference.

16 ' You may seem like a beast or a baboon today, but within ten days you could be a god in their eyes if you would return to your philosophy and reverence reason.

17 ' Don't act as though you'll live to be a thousand. Your days are numbered like everyone else's. In what remains of your allotted time, while you still can, become good.

18 ' How much time and effort a man saves by paying no attention to what his neighbor says or does or thinks, and by concentrating on his own behavior to make it holy and just! The good man isn't looking around for cheaters. He dashes straight for the finish and leans into the tape.

> THE GOOD MAN ISN'T LOOKING AROUND FOR CHEATERS. HE DASHES STRAIGHT FOR THE FINISH AND LEANS INTO THE TAPE.

19 ▸ The man who pants after praise and yearns to "make history" forgets that those who remember him will die soon after he goes to his grave, as will those who succeed the first generation of them that praise him, until after passing from one generation to the next, through many generations, the bright flame of his memory will flutter, fade, and go out. But what if those who praise you never died, and they sang your praises forever? What difference would that make? That the praise will do nothing for you dead isn't my point. What will it do for you now that you're still alive, except perhaps to offer a means to some other end? Meanwhile, you neglect nature's means of achieving the same ends directly while worrying about how you'll be remembered after you're dead.

20 ▸ Whatever is beautiful owes its beauty to itself, and when it dies its beauty dies with it. Praise adds nothing to beauty—makes it neither better nor worse. This is also true for commonly praised objects, natural wonders, for example, or works of art. What does anything that is truly beautiful lack? Nothing! No more than does moral or natural law, truth, kindness, or self-respect. Which of these is improved by praise or marred by criticism? Does an emerald's beauty fade because it is not praised? What about gold, ivory, porphyry, a lyre, a sword, a flower, or a tree?

21 ▸ If souls survive death for all eternity, how can the heavens hold them all? Or for that matter, how can the earth hold all the bodies that have been buried in it? The answers are the same. Just as on earth, with the passage of time, decaying and transmogrified corpses make way for the newly dead, so souls released into the heavens, after a season of flight, begin to break up, burn, and be absorbed back into the womb of reason, leaving room for souls just beginning to fly. This is the answer for those who believe that souls survive death.

When it comes to bodies, we must count not only human remains, but all those animals killed and eaten every day by humans and other species. What a vast number of bodies are buried daily in the earth as well as in the bodies of those who devour the dead! Yet there is plenty of room to contain them, thanks to the body's chemical transformation of the dead into blood and breath and energy.

How can we know what really happens? By distinguishing between material and logical causes.

22 › Stop dithering around. In every confrontation, render what is just; from every impression, extract what is true.

23 › I am in harmony with all that is in harmony with you, O thou great Universe. Nothing opportune for you is too early or too late for me. Anything your seasons bear, O Nature, is fruit of mine; all comes from you, abides in you, and returns to you. If poets can sing "Dear City of Cecrops," will I not say "Dear City of God"?

24 › Democritus said, "If you would be happy, limit your activities to a few." Is it not better simply to do what is necessary and no more, to limit yourself to what reason demands of a social animal and precisely in the manner reason dictates? This adds to the happiness of doing a few things the satisfaction of having done them well. Most of what we say and do is unnecessary anyway; subtract all that lot, and look at the time and contentment you'll gain. On each occasion, therefore, a man should ask himself, "Do I really need to say or do this?" In this way, he will remove not only unnecessary actions, but also the superfluous ideas that inspire needless acts.

25 › A test: try living the life of a good man and see how it suits you—be the man happy with his fate, rejoicing in his acts of justice, and bent on deeds of kindness.

26 › You looked at that side. Now look at this. Calm down. Be simple. Has someone done something wrong? He has wronged himself. Has something happened to you? Fine. Every thread of your life was woven on the great loom of destiny from the beginning. The conclusion? Life is short. Save the moment by doing what is reasonable and right. Be serious, but not with fears and frets and frowns.

27 › Either a universe of transparent orderliness or a labyrinth with a secret design. Otherwise, could disorder reign in the universe while order subsists in you? And at the same time as all things,

existing individual and apart, dance in perfect step with one another?

28 ʾ What a foul character! How unmanly, obstinate, savage! How like a beast or a babe—foolish, false, and unpredictable, grasping and tyrannical!

29 ʾ The man who fails to understand what goes on in the world is as much a stranger to the world as he who is ignorant of how the world is made. He is a fugitive running from the law; a blind man whose eyes cannot see reason; a beggar leaning on others and incapable of standing on his own feet; a pustule on the face of the earth because he has separated himself from the reasonable law that holds the world together by declaring his displeasure with this or that (and forgetting that he too is a "this or that"); an amputated body part, severed from the fellowship of all rational souls, one and indivisible.

30 ʾ There goes a philosopher without a coat, another without a book, yet another half starved saying as he goes, "I have no bread, but still I remain faithful to reason." And here I sit, well nourished and surrounded by my books, unfaithful to reason.

31 ʾ Cherish your gifts, however humble, and take pleasure in them. Spend the rest of your days looking only to the gods from whom comes every good gift and seeing no man as either master or slave.

> CHERISH YOUR GIFTS,
> HOWEVER HUMBLE,
> AND TAKE PLEASURE IN THEM.

32 ʾ Now picture the times of Vespasian. This is what you'll see: men marrying, raising children, getting sick, dying, going to war, partying, engaging in business, farming, flattering, bragging, suspecting, scheming, hoping for others to die, complaining about hard times, making love or wanting to, making money or wanting to,

coveting high office, and seeking to be crowned king. But where is all this teeming life now?

Leap ahead to the times of Trajan, and what will you find? The same, of course, and it too dead and gone. For that matter, examine the history of any people or time. See how hard they strove and how soon they vanished back into the elements from which they were born. But most of all consider those you personally have known who, ignoring the good that lay at their feet, ran after some vain thing and never found the happiness that was within their reach all the time. A man's interest in an object should be no greater than its intrinsic worth. Remember this and you will not become distracted by trivialities or discouraged if you never get around to some of life's details.

33 · Words that everyone once used are now obsolete, and so are the men whose names were once on everyone's lips: Camillus, Caeso, Volesus, Dentatus, and to a lesser degree Scipio and Cato, and yes, even Augustus, Hadrian, and Antoninus are less spoken of now than they were in their own days. For all things fade away, become the stuff of legend, and are soon buried in oblivion. Mind you, this is true only for those who blazed once like bright stars in the firmament, but for the rest, as soon as a few clods of earth cover their corpses, they are "out of sight, out of mind."

In the end, what would you gain from everlasting remembrance? Absolutely nothing. So what is left worth living for? This alone: justice in thought, goodness in action, speech that cannot deceive, and a disposition glad of whatever comes, welcoming it as necessary, as familiar, as flowing from the same source and fountain as yourself.

34 · Gladly put yourself in Clotho's hands and let her weave your thread into the great web of life however she chooses.

35 · Everything disperses and vanishes like smoke, both the rememberer and the remembered.

36 · Look around you and see how everything is perpetually changing, and get used to the idea that nature loves nothing more than to change the things that are and to make more things like them come

into being. In a way, everything is a seed of the thing that grows out of it. Don't be so naive and narrow-minded as to assume that a seed is only something planted in the earth or in a womb.

37 · You will soon be dead, and you are not yet simple, untroubled, free from fears of outside harm, eager to bear the burdens of others, or convinced that honest dealing is always best.

38 · Look deep into the hearts of men, and see what delights and disgusts the wise.

39 · You cannot be harmed by the law of another man's being, nor can any change or alteration in your circumstances hurt you. Where is the injury then? It is in your sense of injury—in the part of you that forms a judgment about such things. Form no judgment, and the injury disappears. Even if what is closest to you, your body, is mutilated and burned, festers and rots, force the part of you that forms an opinion about such things to remain calm and refuse to judge as either good or bad what can as easily happen to a good man as to a bad. For whether a man lives in harmony with nature or not isn't the sole determinant of whether something is for nature or against it.

40 · Never forget that the universe is a single living organism possessed of one substance and one soul, holding all things suspended in a single consciousness and creating all things with a single purpose that they might work together spinning and weaving and knotting whatever comes to pass.

41 · As Epictetus said, "You are but a soul propping up a corpse."

42 · Change is never bad, nor are the effects of change good. This sort of judgment about change, which one hears all the time, is not helpful.

43 · Time is a kind of river, an irresistible flood sweeping up men and events and carrying them headlong, one after the other, to the great sea of being.

44 ' Everything is as natural and familiar as a spring rose or a summer grape. This includes disease, death, slander, treason, and all those things that gladden and sadden the hearts of fools.

45 ' What follows always bears some relation to what came before. Life is not like an arbitrary series of random numbers, but more like a logical progression. Likewise, just as natural objects appear to cooperate and exist in harmony with one another, so too events are not remarkable because of the order in which they happen, but because of their amazing affinity with one another.

46 ' Remember the words of Heraclitus: "Earth dies to become water; water dies to become air; air dies to become fire"; and so on. Remember also "the person who forgets where his path leads," as well as "the person who sets himself apart from his constant companion, the very reason that governs the universe." We must not "speak and act like sleeping men" who have no control over their words and deeds, nor should we behave like "children with parents," doing without question "just what our fathers have told us to do."

47 ' Just imagine the gods saying to you, "Tomorrow, you're going to die, or at the latest, the day after tomorrow." Are you going to make a big deal over the difference between tomorrow and the day after and start begging the gods for an extra day? Not unless you're a thorough-going coward. Really, what's the difference? Well then, take the same attitude toward living to be a ripe old age or dying tomorrow.

48 ' Don't forget how many doctors have died who once furrowed their brows over their patients; how many statisticians who confidently predicted the deaths of millions; how many philosophers after inventing countless theories on death and immortality; how many warriors after slaying thousands of their enemies; how many dictators after exercising their power over life and death with monstrous arrogance, as though they were gods; indeed, how many entire cities have perished: Helike, Pompeii, Herculaneum, and others too numerous to name or know.

Then begin to count up those you have known personally, one by one: how this one buried his friend and was later mourned himself, buried by another—all in so short a time. See how quick and coarse the drama of human life runs: yesterday a mucous membrane; tomorrow an embalmed corpse or a heap of ash. Spend this brief moment walking with nature and greet your short journey's end with a good grace, like the olive that falls to the ground when it is ripe, blessing the earth that receives it and grateful to the tree that bore it.

49 ・ Be like a rocky promontory against which the restless surf continually pounds; it stands fast while the churning sea is lulled to sleep at its feet. I hear you say, "How unlucky that this should happen to me!" Not at all! Say instead, "How lucky that I am not broken by what has happened and am not afraid of what is about to happen. The same blow might have struck anyone, but not many would have absorbed it without capitulation or complaint."

After all, why do we speak of good luck and bad luck anyway? Would you call something that is not contrary to a man's nature a piece of bad luck? And can something be contrary to a man's nature that nature wills? Well, you know perfectly well what nature wills. Do the waves that crash upon you prevent you in any way from being just, forgiving, moderate, discerning, truthful, loyal, free-spirited, and in possession of all the other noble qualities that nature wills for man's well-being? The next time you are tempted to complain of your bad luck, remember to apply this maxim: "Bad luck borne nobly is good luck."

> BAD LUCK
> BORNE NOBLY
> IS GOOD LUCK.

50 ・ A simple but helpful device for mitigating the fear of death is to review the cases of those who once clung tenaciously to life. How are they better off than those who died young? They're all dead now, Cadicianus, Fabius, Julianus, Lepidus and all the others who, after burying many of their friends, were eventually laid to rest themselves. What difference does it make? A few more years filled

with thankless labors and dubious companions and physical infir-
mities. Forget about it, and look instead into the bottomless abyss of
time behind you and at the infinite number of years ahead. By
comparison, what's the difference between three-hundred-year-old
Nestor and a three-day-old babe?

51 · Always run the shortest course, the one laid out by nature.
This will enable you to speak and act sensibly; it will free you from
bickering and petty ambition; and it will remove your anxieties and
affectations.

BOOK FIVE

1 · In the morning, when you can't get out of bed, tell yourself: "I'm getting up to do the work only a man can do. How can I possibly hesitate or complain when I'm about to accomplish the task for which I was born? Was I made for lying warm in bed under a pile of blankets?"

"But I enjoy it here."

Was it for enjoyment you were born? Are you designed to act or to be acted upon? Look at the plants, sparrows, ants, spiders and bees, all busy at their work, the work of welding the world. Why should you hesitate to do your part, the part of a man, by obeying the law of your own nature?

"Yes, but nature allows for rest too."

True, but rest—like eating and drinking—has natural limits. Do you disregard those limits as well? I suppose you do, although when it comes to working, you are quick to look for limits and do as little as possible. You must dislike yourself. Otherwise, you'd like your nature and the limits it imposes. At the same time, you'd recognize that enjoyment is meant to be found in work too and that those who enjoy their work become totally absorbed in it, often forgetting to eat and drink and seek other forms of enjoyment. Do you think less of your life's work than the sculptor does his sculpting, the dancer his dancing, the miser his money, or the star his stardom? They gladly forgo food and sleep to pursue their ends. To you, does the work of building a better society seem less important, less deserving of your devotion?

2 · How easy it is to push away and block out every rude and unwelcome idea, and suddenly to recover one's peace of mind.

3 · Claim your right to say or do anything that accords with nature, and pay no attention to the chatter of your critics. If it is good to say

or do something, then it is even better to be criticized for having said or done it. Others have their own consciences to guide them and will follow their own lights. Don't be gazing after them, but keep your eyes on the straight path ahead of you, the path of your own nature and of the nature of the universe. The path of both is the same.

> IF IT IS GOOD
> TO SAY OR DO SOMETHING,
> THEN IT IS EVEN BETTER
> TO BE CRITICIZED FOR HAVING
> SAID OR DONE IT.

4 ' I walk with nature until the day I fall down and find rest, releasing my last breath into the air from which I drew it and all those that came before, and reposing in the earth from which my father took his seed, my mother her blood, and my nurse her milk, the same earth which has never failed to fill my belly and quench my thirst, which bears my rude tread and endures my rapacious abuse.

5 ' So you don't dazzle them with your blazing intellect. Get over it! Still you have plenty going for you and no reason to make excuses and hold back. Let the virtues you do possess shine forth: your honesty, dignity, and stamina; your indifference to pleasure and loathing of self-pity; your wanting little for yourself and giving much to others; your measured words and temperate deeds. Do you not recognize these as qualities you possess or as virtues you are fully capable of owning? Then why do you hide them behind a mask of false modesty and keep your bright spirit in darkness? What compels you to grumble, grasp, and grovel, to be boastful one moment and to snivel the next, and in the end to lay the blame for so much sorry behavior on either a pathetic body or a confused mind? Good heavens! You could have rid yourself of all this long ago. The only deficiency over which you might lack some measure of control is a certain slowness of mind, a difficulty in grasping ideas quickly, but even this can be remedied through hard training and disciplined study, if you don't ignore it and wallow in your stupidity.

6 · There are three kinds of men in this world. The first, when he helps someone out, makes it known that he expects something in return. The second would never be so bold, but in his mind he knows what he has done and considers the other person to be in his debt. The third somehow doesn't realize what he has done, but he's like a vine that bears its fruit and asks for nothing more than the pleasure of producing grapes. A horse gallops, a dog hunts, a bee makes honey, one man helps another, and the vine bears fruit in due season.

You ought to be like that third fellow, who does good without giving it a second thought.

"What! Are men to be numbered with the lower forms of life that act and are acted upon without awareness? Aren't you always saying that man is a rational animal, and isn't it the mark of a rational animal to realize when he is acting socially and to hope, by God, that his neighbor appreciates it?"

What you say is true, but you've twisted my meaning and are like one of those fellows I discussed earlier, who can't tell the difference between clever argument and good sense. But if you think about it and truly grasp my meaning, never fear that you will fail to meet your social obligations and do good without looking for reward.

7 · A prayer of the Athenians: "Rain, rain, dear Zeus, on the fields and plains of the Athenians." This is how we too should pray— simply and freely—or we should not bother praying at all.

8 · It is common when speaking of a doctor's orders to say: "Aesclepius prescribed for this fellow horseback riding, cold baths, or walking barefoot." In the same way, we should be able to say, "Nature has prescribed a disease, a disfiguration, a dismemberment, or some other disability." In the former case, treatments are prescribed to make a man physically whole, whereas in the latter case, circumstances are prescribed to complete or round out his destiny. These circumstances are like the stones that a stonemason uses to construct a wall or pyramid; they are selected and fit together to form one solid structure. By coming together in the right way all the individual stones become one. Just as the universe is the coming together of all the

objects in it, so destiny is the one compelling and inescapable logic to which every cause contributes. This is expressed even by those who don't fully understand it when they use an expression like "he had it coming." Yes, he did have it coming. Nature prescribed it for him, and he should accept it as readily as he would a doctor's orders. It may even hurt, but he welcomes it in hopes of being well again.

Accept the prescriptions of nature as if they were intended for your own health, even if at times they may seem cruel or disagreeable to you. Remember that they are for the good of the universe and for the pleasure of God. Nothing is prescribed for any part that does not benefit the whole. After all, it would violate the nature of anything to act against its own interests in governing its parts.

There are two reasons, then, for being content with whatever happens to you. The first is that it was meant just for you, prescribed for you, and preserved for you like a thread woven into your destiny from the very beginning. The second is that whatever happens to the individual contributes to the health, wholeness, and survival of the entire universe. You destroy the symmetry and continuity of the whole if you cut away even one part or remove a single cause. And that's what you do, to the extent you're able, every time you whine and complain—mutilate the whole by amputating the parts.

9 · Don't become disgusted with yourself, lose patience, or give up if you sometimes fail to act as your philosophy dictates, but after each setback, return to reason and be content if most of your acts are worthy of a good man. Love the philosophy to which you return, and go back to it, not as an unruly student to the rod of a schoolmaster, but as a sore eye to a sponge and egg whites, or a wound to cleansing ointments and clean bandages. In this way, you will obey the voice of reason not to parade a perfect record, but to secure an inner peace. Remember, philosophy desires only what pleases your nature while you wanted something at odds with nature.

"Precisely, doesn't it all come down to what pleases me most?"

Yes, it does, but be careful. This is just the argument pleasure uses to trick most people. Ask yourself—what could possibly please you more than to be great-souled, free, natural, gentle, and devout? And what is more pleasing than practical wisdom when you consider the reliability and efficiency of knowledge and understanding in every situation?

10 ⋅ Everything is so shrouded in mystery that many philosophers—including some of the best thinkers—believe that knowledge is unattainable. Even Stoics sometimes waver on this point, acknowledging the fallibility of their senses and judgments. Who hasn't at one time or another received a false impression or changed his mind? Then consider the experiences upon which your mind feeds—how short they last, how cheap they are, how likely to be at the mercy of perverts, whores, or thieves. Next, look at the morals and manners of those you live with. No wonder even the best of them is almost unbearable, although no more so than you are to yourself.

In the midst of this darkness and filth, this ruin of time, this decay of substance, of movement and things moved, I cannot begin to know what should win my praise or fire my ambition. Instead, I must find consolation in waiting for my life to end without being irritated at the delay and while taking comfort in knowing, first, that nothing will happen to me that is not a part of nature's plan, and second, that there is no power on earth that can force me to act against the laws of God and the dictates of conscience.

11 ⋅ "How, at this moment, am I using my mind?" This is a question worth asking all the time. So is this: "How do my words and deeds measure up to the ruling reason within me? And who owns this mind of mine anyway? An infant? A boy? A woman? A tyrant? A dumb animal? A wild beast?"

12 ⋅ If you want to understand what sorts of things seem good to a person, try using Menander's famous line ("So surrounded by good things was he . . .") as a test. If he's someone who values real goods—wisdom, for example, self-restraint, justice, and courage—and thinks only of these when he hears the old joke about too much of a good thing, then Menander's line will make no sense to him. But if instead he thinks of the things that seem good to most people, he'll have no trouble appreciating the poet's humor. Everyone understands this difference. If they didn't, they'd find the joke shocking and offen-

sive, but since they know the poet is talking about wealth and the effects of luxury and fame, they think his punch line witty and well put. So, go ahead and ask yourself if you should conceive as good those things that, upon reflection, might inspire someone to say of their owner, "So surrounded by good things was he . . . that he didn't have a place to take a shit."

13 · I am formed out of two elements: the causal and the material. Neither of these will be reduced to nothingness when I am dead, just as neither came out of nothingness when I was born. It follows that each part of me will someday be transformed into a part of the universe, and that part will later be transformed into another part, and so on forever. In just this way, I came into being, as did my parents and their parents and all those who came before them. Nothing contradicts this theory, even if the universe is organized in finite periods.

14 · Reason and logic are governed by their own laws and employ their own methods. They launch themselves at will, and they head straight for their target. This is why we call actions that seem to us reasonable and logical "right," because they are right on target.

15 · Nothing should be called good that fails to enlarge our humanity. This excludes all those things that a man doesn't need in order to be human and that human nature doesn't fit him with or perfect in him. Whatever is excluded by this definition, then, has no bearing on man's purpose in life or on the good that sums up his purpose. Moreover, if any of the so-called good things our definition excludes were really essential to our humanity, why is it that doing without them or opposing them strengthens a man's reputation while showing moderation in their regard is considered "good"? The fact is, the more you free yourself from things of this sort and live happily without them, the more you will enlarge your humanity.

16 · Your mind is colored by the thoughts it feeds upon, for the mind is dyed by ideas and imaginings. Saturate your mind, then, with a succession of ideas like these: Wherever life is possible, it is

possible to live in the right way. What if you live in a palace? Then it is possible to live in a palace in the right way. As I've said before, everything came into being for a purpose and is drawn toward the achievement of its purpose. This purpose is also its end, where both its interest and its good lie. Now, what is good for a rational being is the company of others. It was proven long ago that we are born to enjoy one another and to live together in harmony. What could be clearer than that the lower forms of life are meant to serve the higher, and the higher are meant to serve one another? The living are higher than the lifeless, and the thinking are higher than those that can merely draw breath.

> WHEREVER LIFE IS POSSIBLE,
> IT IS POSSIBLE TO LIVE
> IN THE RIGHT WAY.

17 ' To hope for the impossible is madness, and it is impossible for the wicked not to do wrong.

18 ' Nothing ever happens to a man that he is not equipped by nature to endure. Someone else experiences the same difficulty you have faced, and unaware of what has happened or not wanting to lose face, he remains undaunted and unharmed. Is it not shameful when ignorance and vanity outperform wisdom?

19 ' Worldly circumstances and affairs cannot touch the mind, cannot penetrate it, cannot alter or move it, for the mind alters and moves itself, molding the world in the shape of whatever judgments it pleases the mind to make.

20 ' Other members of the human race are my nearest relations in this respect only—I am obligated to do them good and to be patient with them. But if they prevent me from doing what I know is right, then they become as distant and indifferent to me as the sun, the wind, or a wild beast. Although others may at times hinder me from acting, they cannot control or impede my spirit and my will. Reserving its judgments and adapting to change, my mind bypasses or dis-

places any obstacle in its way. It uses whatever opposes it to achieve its own ends; it turns roadblocks into roads.

21 ' Bow before the greatest power in the universe; it makes use of everything and governs all things well. Reverence the same power in yourself. Born of the same spark, this power in you puts all things to good use and governs your life well.

22 ' What does not hurt the community cannot hurt the individual. Every time you think you've been wronged, apply this rule: if the community isn't hurt by it, then neither am I. But what if the community is hurt? Then don't be angry with the person who caused the injury. Just help him to see his mistake.

23 ' Think often of how rapidly the stuff of existence sweeps past us and is carried out of sight. Being is like a perpetually flooding river, its currents ever changing, its causes numberless and varied. Nothing stands still, not even the water at our feet that plunges into the infinite abyss of the past behind us and the future ahead, plunges and disappears. In this situation, isn't it foolish to put on airs, to strain at the bit, to get all worked up as though any fame or notoriety might last for long?

24 ' Add up the sum of all being and see how microscopic your share of it is; the sum of all time and how infinitesimal your span; and of destiny—what fraction of it is yours?

25 ' Someone wrongs me. Why should I care? That's his business—his inclinations and actions are up to him. I care only about what the universal nature wills for me, and I do what my own nature wills.

> SOMEONE WRONGS ME.
> WHY SHOULD I CARE? THAT'S HIS
> BUSINESS—HIS INCLINATIONS
> AND ACTIONS ARE UP TO HIM.

26 ' Don't let the reasonable guide at the core of your being be swayed by the unconscious movements of the flesh, whether violent or gentle. Don't let it get mixed up with them, but let it stand aloof, confining each sensation to the member for which it is intended. But when the mind, being part of the same organism as the flesh, becomes conscious of these sensations, it should accept them without judging them to be either good or bad.

27 ' Live with the gods! He lives in the company of the gods who hides nothing from them and shows them a man happy with his fate and eager to obey the divine will as revealed by that part of Zeus which the god has given to every man as his ruler and guide—each man's mind and reason.

28 ' Do you get angry with someone for smelling like an old goat? Or for having foul breath? What's the use? Don't all men have armpits and mouths? From these sources, disagreeable odors are bound to arise.

"Okay, but men also have sense and can realize when they're being offensive."

Aren't you clever to think of that! Well, then you must have some sense too. Use your sense to engage his sense. Show him his error, remind him of his offensiveness. If he listens to you, you will cure him with no need for anger.

Don't behave like an actor or a whore.

29 ' There is no reason why you shouldn't live here on earth as you'd like to live in the hereafter. If others won't permit it, then it's time to call it quits and exit this life with grace and equanimity. "The chimney smokes; I'm leaving the room." Why make more of it than that? But as long as nothing drives me from the room, I'm a free man, and no one can keep me from living as I like, which is to conform to the nature of a reasonable and sociable being.

30 ' The cosmic mind is social. It has made the inferior for the superior while fashioning the superior for one another. Notice how it sub-

ordinates some things and coordinates others while giving to each what it truly deserves; see how among the very best there is complete agreement (as all things converge at the pinnacle).

31 ⸰ Until this moment, how have you treated the gods and your parents, brothers, wife, children, teachers, tutors, friends, and relations? Can you honestly say to each of them: "I never wronged you or spoke unkindly of you?" Now that the story of your life is almost told and your long career of public service nears its end, remember all that you have been through, all the heavy burdens you have found the strength to bear. Recall how many beautiful sights you have seen, how many pleasures and pains you have risen above, how many honors you have turned down, how many rude persons you have treated with courtesy.

32 ⸰ Why do the ignorant and uneducated confound the learned and wise? Better to ask, perhaps, who can be learned and wise? Only the one who knows the beginning and the end and discerns the reason that runs through it all and rules the seasons of time and change from eternity.

33 ⸰ Not long and you'll be ashes or bones, and a lingering name. Perhaps not even that. But what's a name anyway? Just a sound, then an echo. All we treasure in life is empty, rotten, and trifling, and we ourselves are no better than puppies snapping at one another. Like children quarrelling, we laugh one moment and burst into tears the next.

Faith and modesty, justice and truth have fled "From Earth's wide bounds to Heaven's heights." Why do you stay behind when you know perfectly well that the world is changing and unstable and your sense of it dim and easily deceived? When the soul is but steam rising from your blood? When being highly regarded in such a place means nothing?

What should I do? Wait calmly for the end, whether it means extinction or metamorphosis. Between now and then, how should I live? How else but by worshipping and blessing the gods and by doing good to others—"bearing their burdens and forbearing their abuse"—and by remembering that whatever dwells in the land of flesh and breath neither belongs to me nor owes me a thing?

34 ・ It is always within your power to prosper provided you are able to choose your path wisely and can think and act in accordance with your choice. God and man, as rational beings, share these two fundamental characteristics: they will resist whatever opposes them, and they will find their true happiness in wanting and doing only what is right.

35 ・ If the wrong is not in me, or the result of something I have done, or harmful to the community—why should it concern me? How can the community be harmed by it anyway?

36 ・ Don't get carried away in your grief over another man's loss, but help him as best you can and as much as his loss deserves. If he has merely lost face or some such, don't act as if some great harm has come to him. That is a bad habit. Instead, think of the old man in the play who begged to have the top he had given his foster-child back, perhaps as a memento, when it came time for the two of them to part, even though he knew perfectly well that it was just a child's toy and nothing more. Ask your friend whom you find publicly mourning his loss, "Have you forgotten what a top is truly worth?"

"Of course not. But it had great sentimental value."

Yes, it appeals to the sentiments of a child. Are you a child?

37 ・ Once I was the luckiest of men, lacking nothing. But what does it mean to have good luck and to lack nothing? It means to have good moods, good desires, and good behavior.

BOOK SIX

1 ' The parts of the whole are docile and adaptable, and in the reason that rules these parts, there exists not the least motive or cause to do wrong. For reason itself contains no evil, makes no mistakes, and inflicts no harm on anything. But as reason dictates, all things come into being and accomplish their appointed ends.

2 ' Do your duty—and never mind whether you are shivering or warm, sleeping on your feet or in your bed, hearing yourself slandered or praised, dying or doing something else. Yes, even dying is an act of life and should be done, like everything else, "to the best of your abilities."

3 ' Look into the heart of the matter. Don't let the essential character or intrinsic worth of anything escape you.

4 ' All material objects are soon transformed, either consumed by fire—if all energy is conserved—or broken into their atoms.

5 ' The sovereign reason knows its own mind, comprehends its work, and understands the material with which it works.

6 ' The best revenge is not to do as they do.

> THE BEST REVENGE
> IS NOT TO DO
> AS THEY DO.

7 ' Let this be your one joy and delight: to go from one act of kindness to another with your mind fixed on God.

8 ' The governing part of the soul is alert to all things, adapts to all things, takes whatever form it fancies, and clothes what lies outside itself in any fashion it chooses.

9 ' Every part of the whole conforms to the nature of the whole and serves the purpose of the whole. This cannot be accomplished if some other nature—either external or internal or existing independently—governs the parts.

10 ' The world is either a mindless binding and loosing of atoms or the unity and order of Providence. If I accept the first scenario, why am I so eager to prolong my days in a body formed by accident and in a world governed by chance? What is the point and purpose of living in such a world other than someday to become dust? And why should even that consideration bother me? All considerations will soon be atomized anyway. But if the other scenario is true, I worship calmly and confidently the Power that rules.

11 ' When you're feeling overwhelmed and confused by the evil in your circumstances or the attacks of your enemies, fall back at once into yourself, while not losing contact with the forces pressing down on you. By thus keeping yourself in harmony with your own nature, you will not only find refreshment but be prepared to win the field.

12 ' If you had both a stepmother and a mother, you would treat your stepmother with respect, but it is your mother to whom you would return again and again. This describes your relationship with the court and with philosophy. Never tire of returning to philosophy and of renewing yourself in her. She makes your life at court more bearable while making you less objectionable to the court.

13 ' Look at fine cuisine and other niceties this way: "Here is the corpse of a fish, there the dead body of a bird or pig; this bottle of vintage Falernian is just grape juice, and that regal robe is only the wool of a lamb soaked in the blood of a shellfish." What about sex-

ual intercourse? "This is the rubbing together of groins and the ejaculation of a sticky liquid accompanied by a spasm." Factual descriptions like these penetrate to the heart of the matter and allow you to see things for what they are. Practice this method of observation throughout your life, and whenever something makes ambitious claims for itself, lay those claims bare by stripping away all the fancy dress and exposing the naked facts. For vanity is the supreme sophist, and when you flatter yourself that you are engaged in some good or worthy enterprise, then you are most easily deceived. (Remember what Crates said about no less a notable than Xenocrates.)

14 ˒ The common sort of person is apt to admire natural objects that fall into one of two broad categories, inanimate objects like wood and stone, or plant life like figs, vines, and olives. The slightly more discerning will admire living creatures like flocks and herds, while the even more refined will prefer products of rational endeavor—not reason itself, mind you, but the effects of reason like the works of artists and craftsmen or the management of a great estate. But the man who puts reason first in order to pursue social and universal ends disregards the rest. He guards his soul by striving to be reasonable in his thoughts and sociable in his actions and by forming common cause with others who would do the same.

15 ˒ Some things are impatient to be born while others are in a hurry to die, and even some part of what is just being born is dying or dead already. As the uninterrupted flow of time replenishes the vast cistern of eternity, so flux and change continually renew the world. In this swollen river, with nothing solid on which to stand, how is a man to know which of the things swirling past him deserve his attention? It is like asking him to win the love of a sparrow that flits past and is already out of sight. That's life—steam rising from the blood, air escaping from the lungs. Just as you draw your breath this moment from the same air into which you will soon release it, so it is with your entire respiratory system—you acquired it yesterday or the day before from the same source to which you will return it tomorrow.

16 ˒ What then deserves our attention, invites our admiration? Surely not the life we have in common with plants or the breath we share with cattle and wild beasts; not the impressions we receive through our senses or the desires that have us dancing on strings; not the need to live in herds or to feed ourselves, a bodily function on the same level as defecating.

What then? The clapping of hands? No, and not men's praise either, for praise is merely a clapping of tongues. But without glory and honor, what's left? Just this: to act or not to act according to the needs and dictates of your own constitution. This is the same guiding principle we find in every art and technology, the aim of which is to perform precisely the task for which it was created. This aim is no different for the vine dresser, the horse breaker, and the dog trainer. What other aim could there be for the art of raising children or the technique of teaching them? This then is what deserves your attention.

Attend to this, and nothing else will matter. But what if you continue to hanker after other things as well? Then don't expect to be free or fulfilled or content. Instead you will be haunted by fear and envy—suspicious of those who might rob you of what you have and scheming against those who have what you want. In short, the man who always wants something else will be filled with turmoil and probably end up blaming the gods. But if you respect and honor the dictates of your own constitution, you will be at peace with yourself, in sweet accord with your fellow man, and in harmony with the gods, pleased with whatever they have arranged and ordained.

17 ˒ The elements appear to move upward or downward or in circles, but the motion of virtue is nothing like this. More divine somehow, virtue advances in ways difficult to measure or discern.

18 ˒ This is what they do. They refuse to be generous in their opinions of their neighbors and contemporaries, but at the same time they want to be held in the highest esteem by those who aren't born yet, yes, even by those whom they have never seen and never will see. It comes pretty close to complaining because your ancestors failed to sing your praises!

19 ˙ Just because you find the work too hard to do, don't leap to the conclusion that it is humanly impossible; but if the work can and should be done by a man, then consider yourself capable of doing it.

20 ˙ If someone accidentally scratches us with his nails or butts us with his head when we're working out in the gym, we don't make a fuss, or strike back in anger, or suspect him of intending to do us future harm. At the same time, we'll probably give him a wide berth, not out of hostility or suspicion, but with good-natured circumspection. Apply this principle outside the gym, and cut life's sparring partners some slack. You can always avoid them, as I said, without suspecting or hating them.

21 ˙ Persuade me or prove to me that I am mistaken in thought or deed, and I will gladly change—for it is the truth I seek, and the truth never harmed anyone. Harm comes from persisting in error and clinging to ignorance.

22 ˙ I do what is expected of me and let nothing get in my way—neither the inanimate, nor the irrational, nor the hopelessly lost.

23 ˙ You possess reason. So use dumb animals and material objects as a reasonable man should—with a generous and free spirit. With other reasonable men, be a good neighbor. And in all things pray for God's guidance without worrying about how long it takes. Even three hours in prayer is worth it.

24 ˙ Death brought Alexander of Macedon and his stable boy to the same end. Either they returned to the great womb from which all things are born, or they disintegrated and scattered into indistinguishable atoms.

25 ˙ Reflect on how much is happening at any given moment in the mental and physical parts of each individual, and you will not wonder at how much more is happening within the same sliver of time in that one boundless whole we call the universe.

26 ' Suppose someone asks, "How do you spell *Antoninus?*" Will you shout out each letter? And if this makes him angry, will you be angry with him in return? Won't you spell the name calmly instead, saying the letters in the right order one by one? Just so, on this earth each task is accomplished by following certain steps. You must know and reverence these steps without becoming agitated or striking out at those who oppose you, and in this way proceed methodically toward your goal.

27 ' Is it not a heartless thing to prevent others from doing what they think is in their own best interest? Yet you do precisely this when you become upset with them for their wrongdoing. After all, what you would forbid as wrong, they believe to be in their interest and to their advantage. "But they are mistaken!" Fine. Then teach them where their true interests lie, but don't fume and fuss and fret.

28 ' Death frees us from the feigning of our senses, the tyranny of our passions, the vagaries of thought, the bondage of desire.

29 ' How shameful and absurd it is for the spirit to surrender when the body is able to fight on!

30 ' Don't be a Caesar drunk with power and self-importance: it happens all too easily. Keep yourself simple, good, pure, sincere, natural, just, god-fearing, kind, affectionate, and devoted to your duty. Strive to be the man your training in philosophy prepared you to be. Fear God; serve mankind. Life is short; the only good fruit to be harvested in this earthly realm requires a pious disposition and charitable behavior.

In all things, show yourself to be the faithful student of Antoninus, who never tired of living in complete accord with reason, acting with moderation on all occasions, controlling even the expressions on his face. Be worthy of his sweetness and devotion, his indifference to praise, his love of putting things in order. Remember how he never abandoned a subject until he had studied it in depth and understood it thoroughly; how he put up with unjustified accusations without saying a word; how he never acted in haste or listened to slander; how he weighed carefully a man's character and actions; how he was never spiteful, craven, suspicious, or pedantic; how simple were his tastes and spare his needs in lodging and bed and dress and food and service; and how he loved hard work and bore the inconveniences and irritations of life with inexhaustible patience.

O, what a man he was! He could work in one place from morning till night without pausing for nourishment or rest and without relieving himself before the usual hour. He was a loyal and steadfast friend, who encouraged plainspoken disagreement with his opinions and delighted in being shown a better way. Finally, he was devout without being in the least superstitious. Remember all this so that in your final hour you too can depart this life with as clear a conscience as his.

31 ‧ Come round, put yourself together, wake up! Admit that what's troubling you are dreams, the products of a lively imagination. Start to see things for what they are again.

32 ‧ I am a mind and a body. To my body, all things are indifferent, since it has no power in itself to discern or influence them. To my mind, all things are likewise indifferent, except for those things of which the mind is conscious. Even among those few things, it is concerned only with the present, being at this moment indifferent to whatever it acted upon in the past or will act upon in the future.

33 ‧ A pain in the hand or in the foot is not contrary to nature so long as it is acquired while the foot is performing the function of feet and the hand is doing the work of hands. By the same token, human suffering is not contrary to nature so long as it arises out of human toil and endeavor. And if it is not contrary to nature, how can suffering then be bad for us?

34 ‧ What manifold pleasures titillate pirates, playboys, parricides, and potentates!

35 ⸱ Look at the experts. Each practices a science or an art with its own standards and principles which he refuses to relinquish, even if he must compromise them on occasion to explain himself or adapt his practice to the non-expert. What a shame that the architect and physician show more allegiance to the principles and standards of their crafts than men do to those principles and standards of right thought and action which they share with the gods!

36 ⸱ In the great universe, Asia and Europe are but small corners, the ocean a drop of water, Mount Athos a handful of dirt, all of modern times a heartbeat in eternity. Everything in this life is infinitesimal, unstable, and fleeting. It all has one source and flows from one universal spring either directly or by secondary and tertiary streams. Even the lion's gaping maw, deadly poison, every harmful and hideous thing you can imagine—whether a thorn or a pestilential swamp— originates from one good and beautiful source. Don't get the idea that this has nothing to do with the One you worship; reflect instead on the gushing fount from which all things flow.

37 ⸱ If you have seen the present, you have seen everything that was and all that will be, world without end; for it all rises from the same source and takes the same form.

38 ⸱ Take time to meditate on the interdependency of everything in the universe. How all things embrace one another, as if they were dear friends. How they defer to one another and form a sweet accord in obedience to the laws of nature.

39 ⸱ Live in harmony with everything around you, and love— without reservations or conditions—those with whom you live and work.

40 ⸱ The manufacturer doesn't need to be present for his machine, instrument, or tool to be used properly. He is, so to speak, outside and apart from it. The same cannot be said of nature and its products. The creative force is a part of everything it produces. This should cause us to revere nature all the more, as well as to realize that by

thinking and acting in accord with nature's design and will, we tap into the mind of this creative force. The cosmic mind is as much a part of us, then, as it is of the universe, and all the power and knowledge available in the universe are accessible to the man who lives in perfect harmony with nature.

41 ˙ If you consider things outside your control as good or bad, then whenever something bad happens or something good fails to materialize, you blame the gods or are angry with men because they are, or could be, or someday might be responsible for the presence of some evil or the absence of some good. This sort of thinking breeds injustice. If, on the other hand, you think of only those things under your control as good or bad, then you will have no cause to find fault with God and no reason to quarrel with others.

42 ˙ All of us are working together toward one great end, some knowingly and purposefully, others blindly. I think it was Heraclitus who said that even in our sleep we labor to build the world. Everyone participates in his own way, critics included, as well as those who dig in their heels and imagine they are resisting change— the world needs us all. So choose your side. But know this, whatever side you choose, the One who governs all will know perfectly well how to put you to good use and position you amongst his workers. Be sure, in this great drama, to be more than a throw-away line or a coarse jest.

43 ˙ Does the sun aspire to do the rain's work, or Asclepius the job of a fertility goddess? Are the stars not all different, yet all cooperating to the same end?

44 ˙ If the gods had a hand in designing my fate, they did well: it is hard to imagine a malevolent god. Why would they harm me anyway? How could hurting me serve the interests of the universe, their primary concern? Yet even if they had nothing to do with my particular fate, they certainly shaped the universe, and I am bound to accept and respect their handiwork. To think other than this would be impious, and in that case, we might just as well do away

with sacrifices, prayers, and oaths, and all the other religious observances we perform believing that the gods are present and interested in us.

But suppose, just for the sake of argument, that the gods are indifferent to our fate as well as the fate of the universe. I am still here, and I must still consider my own interest. What is that interest unless it is to conform to my nature and obey the laws of my being? These things I can know about my nature and the laws governing it: that I can reason and that I cannot exist alone, without the company and cooperation of others. As Antoninus, my city and country is Rome; as a man, the world is my home. Whatever improves and benefits these is good for me.

45 ﹐ Whatever happens to a particular individual is good for society as a whole. Not only this, but if you look closely, you will see that what is good for one benefits others as well. To understand this, you must think of "good" in utilitarian rather than in moral terms.

46 ﹐ Just as circus games and other popular entertainments offer the same tedious scenes over and over, so it is with life—an appalling sameness, a tiresome round of cause and effect. When will it ever end?

47 ﹐ Think continually of those who are dead—men of all kinds, classes, and vocations, down to houseboys like Philistion, Phoebus, and Origanion. Read down the endless list on which our names too will soon appear beside those of dazzling orators and sober philosophers—Heraclitus, Pythagoras, and Socrates—and along with the host of heroes before them, and the kings and captains who came after. To their ranks add Eudoxus, Hipparchus, Archimedes, and other noble natures, penetrating intellects, indefatigable workers, imposters, bullies, and those, like Menippus and his kind, who laugh and joke about the littleness of life and the shortness of breath. Think of it. All of these men laid to rest so long ago. What did they—and all those we've never heard of—hope to win from this life? Life's one prize is in seeking truth and doing justice and being charitable even to those who lie and cheat.

48 ⋅ When your spirits need a lift, think of the virtues and talents of those around you—one's energy, another's modesty, the generosity of a third, something else in a fourth. Nothing is so inspiring or uplifting as the sight of these splendid qualities in our friends. Keep them always in mind.

49 ⋅ Are you unhappy with what you weigh? Would you like to be fatter, say, three hundred pounds? No? Then why do you want to add to the length of your life? Be content with what you have.

50 ⋅ Try to persuade others and bring them along, but act, whether they like it or not, whenever reason or justice demands. If they throw up barriers or use force to stop you, remain calm and welcome their opposition as an opportunity to practice the virtues of patience and self-control. Remember that your abilities to reason and to discern right from wrong are not infallible and that you are not called upon to do the impossible. What is expected from you? The very actions you have taken. By taking them, you have reached your goal and achieved your purpose. Know that in time those things toward which we move come to be.

51 ⋅ The happiness of those who want to be popular depends on others; the happiness of those who seek pleasure fluctuates with moods outside their control; but the happiness of the wise grows out of their own free acts.

52 ⋅ You always own the option of having no opinion. There is never any need to get worked up or to trouble your soul about things you can't control. These things are not asking to be judged by you. Leave them alone.

> YOU ALWAYS OWN
> THE OPTION OF HAVING
> NO OPINION.

53 ⋅ Learn to concentrate on what those around you are saying. Enter as deeply as possible into the mind of each speaker.

54 ⟩ What is useless for the hive is of no use to the bee.

55 ⟩ If sailors won't listen to the ship's captain or patients to their doctor, who will bring the ship into safe haven or heal the sick?

56 ⟩ Imagine among all of those with whom I came into this world how many have already left it!

57 ⟩ Honey tastes bitter to people with jaundice. Those infected with rabies are overcome by fear. And to little boys, a ball is a priceless treasure. So why do I lose my temper? Do errors in judgment exercise any less control over us than bile in the jaundiced or virus in the rabid?

58 ⟩ No one can stop you from obeying the laws of your being, and nothing will happen to you that nature does not approve.

59 ⟩ Who are we trying to please? What do we hope to gain? What are we willing to put ourselves through for it? Yet all trace of this is soon rubbed out by time. How much memory has time already erased!

BOOK SEVEN

1 · What is evil? You have looked on it often, so whatever happens, remind yourself that you have seen it all before. Up and down the stages of history—ancient, medieval, and modern—in great cities and humble households, you will see the same scenes played out. None of them new. All fleeting; all familiar.

2 · How can the general rules by which we live perish unless the particular circumstances which they govern cease to be? It is up to you to keep those circumstances alive by continually recalling what they are. On any subject, you are thereby capable of forming the right opinion and of making a sound judgment, so why should you be afraid? If it cannot be brought to mind, it need not concern you. Understand this and you have nothing to fear. It is in your power to restore life simply by reviewing the life you've lived. This is what it means to live again.

3 · Empty pomp; stage plays; flocks of sheep and herds of cows; mock battles; a bone flung to lap-dogs; a breadcrumb tossed into a fishpond; the ceaseless toil of ants bearing their burdens; the flight of frightened mice; puppets dancing on their strings—such is life. Your job is to take your place amidst it all with a mild manner and without condescension. Bear in mind that the measure of a man is the worth of the things he cares about.

> BEAR IN MIND THAT THE MEASURE OF A MAN IS THE WORTH OF THE THINGS HE CARES ABOUT.

4 • Weigh each word being said; watch every move being made. In action, figure out the aim of each move. In speech, know the meaning of every word.

5 • Is my mind up to this task or not? If it is, I shall use it to do the work as one would a tool supplied by nature. If not, I will leave the job to someone better able to accomplish it, or if that is not possible, I will do it as best I can with the help of someone who, with my guidance and support, can complete a timely and useful work for the community. But in whatever I do, whether on my own or with someone else, my one objective will be this and only this: to benefit and to live in harmony with the community.

6 • How many once-sung heroes are consigned to oblivion; how many singers of their praises are no more!

7 • Don't be ashamed to ask for help. Take on life's tasks with the resolve of a soldier storming the breach. So what if you are lame and cannot scale the wall alone. Does your lameness prevent you from finding someone to help you?

8 • Don't fear the future. You will face it, if that is your fate, armed with the same reason that protects and guides you in the present.

9 • All things are woven together, and they make a sacred pattern. One might almost say that no one thing is entirely at odds with any other thing. All the parts are arranged in relation to one another, and together they form one beautiful and orderly whole. For there is one universe made out of all things, one God pervading it all, one being and one law, one reason common to all intelligent creatures, and one truth—if creatures sharing similar origins and the same reason can be said to partake of one idea of perfection.

10 • Universal being soon swallows up its material children; universal reason quickly reclaims its lost causes; and buried in eternity is the memory of it all.

11 · To a rational creature, natural acts are also reasonable ones.

12 · Straight, or set straight?

13 · Rational creatures are to one another as body parts are to a single organism. Reason enjoins them to cooperate in pursuit of a single aim. This idea will strike closer to home the more you remind yourself, "I am a body part in the single organism of all intelligent life." But in saying this, in describing yourself as a mere part (*meros*) rather than as an integral member (*melos*), you show that you don't yet love men from the heart; you don't yet take delight in doing them good without consideration of their deserving or your reward. Doing good to others is still a duty, not yet a service unto yourself.

14 · Let come what may to those who are affected by outward circumstance. They will always find something to complain about. For myself, if I choose not to view whatever happens as evil, no harm will come to me. And I can so choose.

> IF I CHOOSE NOT TO VIEW
> WHATEVER HAPPENS AS EVIL,
> NO HARM WILL COME TO ME.
> AND I CAN SO CHOOSE.

15 · No matter what anyone else does or says, I must be good. It is as if gold or an emerald or purple dye were perpetually telling itself, "No matter what anyone may do or say, I must be an emerald and keep my color."

16 · My mind, as an instrument of reason, doesn't invent its own trouble, doesn't frighten or seduce itself. If there is something else that can frighten or harm me, then let it be so, but under no circumstance will the assumptions and imaginings of my own mind lead me to feel fear or pain.

Let the body guard itself against pain, and if it suffers, let its parts proclaim it. But the mind that alone can apprehend fear and pain does not itself suffer and is not inclined to acknowledge either.

The mind, as an instrument of reason, lacks nothing, except what it might imagine itself to lack. Consequently, if it refuses to create troubles and impediments for itself, it cannot be troubled or impeded.

17 ' Happiness is the inner deity, the goodness of pure mind. "What are you doing here, Imagination?! Get out, in God's name, by whatever way you came in. I don't need you. You're just a bad, old habit. Really, I'm not angry with you; I just want you to go."

18 ' Is it change that you fear? But what can happen without it? What is dearer to nature or more vital to the universe? Look at everything that sustains you. Can you take a warm bath if the wood you burn to heat the water doesn't change? Can you digest your food if it doesn't change? Can any of your needs be met without change? Don't you see, then, that the change resulting in your death is no different and similarly feeds the life of the universe?

19 ' Being is like a violent mountain stream in which every part shares the same watery nature and cooperates in the torrential activity of the whole, as do the members of our body with one another. Consider how many a Chrysippus, a Socrates, an Epictetus time has already engulfed and swept away! Whatever your business, whoever you're dealing with, remember how similar, transient, and integral everything is.

20 ' One thing alone troubles me: the thought that I might do what my true self does not will or that I might do what it wills in the wrong way or at the wrong time.

21 ' Soon you will have forgotten everything, and everyone will have forgotten you.

22 ' It is within a man's power to love even those who sin against him. This becomes possible when you realize that they are your brothers, that they wrong you unintentionally or out of ignorance, that in a little while you and they will be dead, and above all, that

they have not really hurt you so long as you have not sullied your conscience or damaged your inner self by responding in kind.

23 ' Nature treats matter like wax, fashioning first a horse, then melting it down and using the same matter to form a tree, then a man, and later something else—each in turn existing for but an instant. Why should the dismantling of a box be any more threatening than its assembling?

24 ' Angry looks offend against nature. From the face that habitually wears a frown, beauty fades and in the end vanishes beyond hope of ever being restored. From this fact try to understand what is contrary to reason: once awareness of sin is lost, what hope is there to go on living?

25 ' Everything you see will soon be transformed by nature into something new, and that in turn will be changed into something newer, and that again into something newer still, that this ancient earth might be forever young.

26 ' When someone wrongs you, ask yourself: What made him do it? Once you understand his concept of good and evil, you'll feel sorry for him and cease to be either amazed or angry. If his concept is similar to yours, then you are bound to forgive him since you would have acted as he did in similar circumstances. But if you do not share his ideas of good and evil, then you should find it even easier to overlook the wrongs of someone who is confused and in a moral muddle.

27 ' Don't hanker after what you don't have. Instead, fix your attentions on the finest and best that you have, and imagine how much you would long for these if they weren't in your possession. At the same time, don't become so attached to these things that you would be distraught if you were to lose them.

28 ' Seek refuge in yourself. The knowledge of having acted justly is all your reasoning inner self needs to be fully content and at peace with itself.

29 ・ Stop fantasizing! Cut the strings of desire that keep you dancing like a puppet. Draw a circle around the present moment. Recognize what is happening either to you or to someone else. Dissect everything into its causal and material elements. Ponder your final hour. Leave the wrong with the person who did it.

> CUT THE STRINGS
> OF DESIRE
> THAT KEEP YOU DANCING
> LIKE A PUPPET.

30 ・ Focus on what is being said. Enter with your mind into what is being done and into the mind of the person doing it.

31 ・ Let your face shine with simplicity, modesty, and indifference to whatever is neither virtue nor vice. Love your fellow man. Walk with God. "All things are governed by laws," said Democritus. It is enough to remember that there are but two laws: the moral laws of the gods and the physical laws of the atoms. These two are sufficient.

32 ・ On death: If the universe is composed only of diverse atoms, death is dispersion; if the universe is really one unified whole, death is extinction or transfiguration.

33 ・ On pain: Unbearable pains end in death; those that linger and persist are bearable. The mind remains calm by withdrawing from the body, and the inviolable inner self is not diminished in any way. Let the dumb body parts affected by the pain make complaint or plead their case, if they can.

34 ・ On fame: Look at the minds of those who crave renown, what they run from, what they chase after. As sand by the sea is continually drifting and covering old dunes with new ones, so in life former glories are quickly hidden by those that come after.

35 · "Do you imagine that a man with true greatness of soul, someone with a vision of all time and a grasp of all things, attaches much importance to the short life of a single person?"

"Impossible," he answered.

"Will the thought of death terrify such a man?"

"Not in the least!"

(From Plato)

36 · "It is the fate of kings to do men good and to be hated for it."

(From Antisthenes)

37 · What a shame—that the mind can command the face to assume whatever look or expression it pleases, but cannot command itself and govern its own thoughts.

38 · "Things upset you? Why? It's nothing to them."

(From Euripides' *Bellerophon*)

39 · "To the deathless gods and to us, bring joy."

(From an unknown poet)

40 · "Lives cut down like ripened corn.
This one passed over; that one shorn."

(From Euripides' *Hypsipyle*)

41 · "Even the gods' terrible neglect of me and my sons
Must have its reason too."

(From Euripides' *Antiope*)

42 · "Goodness and justice side with me."

(From Aristophanes' *Acharnians*)

43 · "Not wailing with the grief-stricken, not quaking with the fearful."

(From an unknown poet)

44 ⸱ "I might in all fairness reply by saying, 'You are wrong, my friend, if you think that a man who is worth anything weighs his chances of living or dying when deciding what to do. No, he considers only whether the action he is about to take is just or unjust, the work of a good man or bad.'"

(From Plato's *Apology,* the words of Socrates)

45 ⸱ "As I see it, my fellow Athenians, here's how it is: wherever a man takes his stand, whether in accord with his own best judgment or in obedience to his commander's orders, that's where he needs to plant his feet and face every danger, careless of death and of everything but dishonor."

(From Plato's *Apology,* the words of Socrates)

46 ⸱ "But consider, my good friend, whether to be noble and good may require something other than preserving your own skin or saving someone else's. Won't the real man dismiss any consideration of how long he may live and, not clutching at life, be happy to leave this up to God? Won't he accept the saying of women that 'no one ever escaped his fate' and then go on to examine how best to live in whatever time he has left?"

(From Plato's *Gorgias*)

47 ⸱ Fly with the stars in their courses, and swim among the ever-changing elements in their fluid transmutations. Imaginings like these will wash away the filth and grime of this earthbound existence.

48 ⸱ According to a lovely saying by Plato, anyone who aspires to make observations about mankind should look upon the human scene as from some lofty height—herds, armies, farms, weddings and divorces, births and deaths, the cacophony of law courts and the stillness of wilderness areas, peoples of every hue and stamp, celebrating and mourning, buying and selling: the harmonious hodgepodge of life, the order built of opposites.

49 ⸱ Look at the past with its endless succession of empires, and you see the future. The two are the same since there is no way of escaping

the changeless rhythm of the present. Study man for forty years or for ten thousand—it's all the same. What more can you expect to see?

50 ‧ "What earth bears is to earth borne back,
    And what grows from celestial seed
    Is harvested in the heavens"
        (from Euripides' *Chrysippus,* the words of Anaxagoras)

—in other words, the bonds of matter melt away and the basic elements disperse.

51 ‧ Also:

    "Trying with food and drink and magic spells
    To dam life's natural flow and not to die."
        (From Euripides' *Suppliants*)

Or:

    "Feeling God's headwind beating on our backs,
    We pull harder at our oars and make no complaint."
        (From an unknown poet)

52 ‧ "Faster to the takedown," he may be a better wrestler, but not more public-spirited, modest-minded, prepared to meet the whims of fate, kindly disposed to those who err or offend.

53 ‧ When a good work can be accomplished by using the same reason common to both men and gods, you have nothing to fear. When you can be of service by doing something well and in keeping with the law of your being, no harm will come to you.

54 ‧ It is within your power, always and everywhere, to be content with what the gods have given you, to deal justly with people as you find them, and to guard your thoughts against the intrusion of untested or inchoate ideas.

55 ' Don't look to the actions and opinions of others for guidance, but fix your eyes on nature which reveals both the nature of the circumstances surrounding you and the nature of what you need to do. Each person must act as the law of his being dictates: irrational beings are made for rational beings and constituted in such a way that in each instance the inferior serves the interests of the superior, while rational beings are made for one another. The first law of man's being, then, is his sense of kinship.

Following close behind, the second law is his resistance to physical forms of persuasion. Reasonable and intelligent men define their own limits and are not moved beyond them by exterior forces or interior instincts. These influence us as they do animals, but our intellect will seek to rule and not be made subject to them, and this is as it should be, since the law of our being declares that we are to use—and not be used by—them.

The third law of a rational being is resistance to haste and deception. Let the well-ordered mind obey these three laws and not deviate from this path, and it will take possession of all that belongs to it.

56 ' Imagine that you have died and have received the gift of a new life. Live it, full of wondrous gratitude, in sweet accord with nature.

57 ' Cherish the life you have been given and all that is woven into your destiny, but no more. After all, what could suit you better?

58 ' In every crisis, bear in mind the examples of those who in similar circumstances lost control of themselves, were taken by surprise, or complained bitterly. Where did their actions get them? Nowhere. Do you want to end up in the same place? Why not leave these emotional outbursts to those who are controlled or distracted by them? Concentrate instead on taking advantage of the crisis, using it as raw material with which to build something beautiful and good. Just remember that in the end you must approve of your own actions and that the aim of the action also matters.

59 ' Dig down within yourself. The fount of goodness lies within and will keep flowing as long as you keep digging.

60 ▸ Whether standing or reclining, control the body's posture by not slouching or sprawling. Just as you can read a person's intelligence and character in his face, you can see them in the way he holds his body. But these appearances should be preserved without conscious effort.

61 ▸ Living is more like wrestling than dancing: you have to stay on your feet, ready and unruffled, while blows are being rained down on you, sometimes from unexpected quarters.

62 ▸ Reflect carefully on those whose good opinion you covet and on what motivates them. If you examine the reasons for their likes and dislikes, you will not blame them for failing to speak well of you, nor will their praise mean that much to you.

63 ▸ "No one," said Plato, "knowingly chooses to live without the truth." Or without justice, wisdom, compassion, and the like. Keep this thought perpetually in mind, and you will treat everyone more gently.

64 ▸ Whenever you suffer pain, keep this thought handy: pain is nothing to be ashamed of, nor can it impair your mind, at least not the mind's ability to reason and to fulfill its social obligations. In most cases the words of Epicurus will help you: "Pain is never unbearable or unending, so long as you are mindful of its limits and bridle your imagination." Remember too that many of life's little discomforts and irritants, although we do not recognize it, are mild forms of pain—drowsiness, for example, or feverishness or loss of appetite. Whenever you are attacked by one of these, say to yourself: "I am surrendering to pain."

65 ▸ Do not feel for misanthropes what they feel for mankind.

66 ▸ How do we know that Telauges (Pythagoras' son) was not a better man than Socrates? It proves nothing to say that Socrates died a more glorious death, or debated more adroitly with the sophists, or showed more toughness in mounting the guard on a frosty night; or

that he valiantly disobeyed the order to arrest Leo the Salaminian, or that he "walked with his nose in the air." Although we may doubt this last report of Aristophanes, all of these considerations are really beside the point, which is: What sort of soul did Socrates possess? Did he find happiness in treating others fairly and in showing reverence to the gods? Or did he allow the wickedness of others to exasperate him and their ignorance to enslave him? Did he accept his lot in life, regarding it not as something unnatural or intolerable, while preserving his mind from the passions of the body?

67 ⟡ Nature did not join the mind to the body so thoroughly that the mind cannot know itself apart from the body and rule what belongs to it. Never forget this, and remember too on how little your happiness depends. You may not have what it takes to be a profound thinker or a brilliant scientist, but you can still be a free man who respects himself, gives generously to others, and obeys God. It is even possible to be godlike without being recognized for these divine attributes.

68 ⟡ Live freely and joyfully even if you are surrounded by those who plot and shout against you, even if wild beasts claw away the soft clay that encases you. In the midst of all this, what prevents the mind from remaining calm, sizing up the situation correctly, and seizing whatever opportunities present themselves? Now your theoretical judgment will say, "This is the reality of the situation regardless of what others may think or say," and your practical sense will say to the opportunities that arise, "There you are. I was looking for you." For every moment provides us with opportunities to exercise the virtues of neighborliness and thought, or in other words, to practice the art of being human and divine. All that happens is of use to gods or men; nothing is new or unmanageable; everything is familiar and serviceable.

69 ⟡ To live each day as if it were your last without speeding up or slowing down or pretending to be other than what you are—this is perfection of character.

70 ᛫ You don't hear the gods, who must endure forever, complaining about all the nonsense they have had to put up with at the hands of so many worthless creatures. On the contrary, they look after them in a thousand different ways. So by what right do you, whose end is just a few heartbeats away, grow weary and make excuses, you who are yourself one of those worthless creatures?

71 ᛫ How ridiculous not to avoid wronging others, which I have the power to do, while wishing to avoid being wronged by others whose actions are beyond my control!

72 ᛫ Whatever your reasoning and social faculty finds unintelligent or unneighborly, it rightly judges to be inferior to itself.

73 ᛫ When you have done something well and someone else has benefited from it, why do you crave yet a third reward, as fools do, who want to be thanked or to be repaid?

74 ᛫ No one tires of being helped, and acts that are consistent with nature, like helping others, are their own reward. How then can you grow tired of helping others when by doing so you help yourself?

75 ᛫ Once universal nature decided to create a world, the slightest subsequent event became the logical and necessary consequence of that original impulse. Otherwise, even the most monumental events bearing the stamp of universal reason are fundamentally unintelligible. Remember this and you will remain calm in the face of life's little ups and downs.

BOOK EIGHT

1 · Here's a thought that should flatten any false pride: it is no longer possible to live your entire life, not even your adult life, as a philosopher. How far short of philosophy you fall is plain to others, as it is to yourself. Your life is flawed, your reputation tainted, and it is no longer possible to win the glory of being a philosopher. Even your calling in life militates against it. Having seen these truths with your own eyes, stop worrying about what others may think and be content to live the rest of your life, as long or short as it may be, according to the requirements of your own nature. Know those requirements well and let nothing pry you from them.

You have searched everywhere, and in all your wanderings you have not found happiness—not in clever arguments, nor in wealth, fame, pleasure, or anything else. Where is happiness then? In doing what a man's nature requires. And how will you do this? By basing your actions and desires on sound principles. What principles? Principles that distinguish right from wrong and demonstrate that nothing is good for a man unless it helps him to be just, responsible, courageous, and free, while nothing is bad that fails to produce the opposite result.

2 · Before you act, ask yourself: "What are the likely consequences of this act? Will I later have cause to regret it?" A little while and I will be dead and all will be gone and forgotten. What more can I ask if I am to act as a rational being in kinship with my fellow man and subject to the same law as God?

3 · Alexander the Great, Julius Caesar, Pompey the Great—what are they compared to Diogenes, Heraclitus, and Socrates? The latter saw into the nature of things, their causes, and their constituent parts, and what is more, the reason that guided them was their own; whereas in

the case of the former, how great the things for which they were responsible and how petty the things to which they were enslaved!

4 · You may explode in rage, but men will still go on doing what they have always done.

5 · Above all, there's no point in worrying. All things obey the laws of nature, and before long you too will be like Hadrian and Augustus—nobody and nowhere. Then, concentrate on the work at hand, seeing it for what it is and bearing in mind your duty to be a good man. Go where your nature takes you without so much as turning in your tracks. Speak what seems to you most just, but don't be rude, arrogant, or pretentious about it.

6 · This is nature's job: to move things from one place to another, to transform them, to take what is here and carry it over there. All is change, yet there's nothing unexpected to fear. All is familiar habit, and every transfer equitable.

7 · Every nature finds fulfillment in pursuing the right path. For a nature like yours endowed with reason, this means refusing to approve ideas that are false or foggy, directing your energies only to the common good, limiting your likes and dislikes to those things that lie within your grasp, and rejoicing in everything the universal nature has assigned you. For your reasonable nature is a part of the universal nature, just as a leaf's nature is part of the plant's, except that a leaf's nature is part of a nature devoid of feeling, deprived of reason, and subject to being hindered, while human nature is part of the universal nature that is unhindered, mindful, and just—demonstrated by the manner in which it assigns to all men according to their worth a fair share of time, substance, cause, activity, and conditions. But don't go looking for equality in individual cases; rather make your comparisons by examining large samples and total outcomes.

8 · "My student days are over!" Nevertheless, you can still learn to check your arrogance, learn to rise above pleasure and pain, learn to

ignore flattery, and learn not only to keep from being upset with the gauche and ungrateful, but to give them a helping hand!

9 ‣ No one should ever hear you complaining about palace life, no one, not even your own ears.

10 ‣ Regret is what we feel when we blame ourselves for failing to take advantage of a useful opportunity. Now, whatever is good is necessarily useful and of pressing concern to every good man, but no such man feels any regret for failing to indulge in a pleasure. Pleasure, therefore, is neither useful nor good.

11 ‣ Ask this of a thing: What is it in and of itself? What is its individual make-up? its essence, form, and matter? its purpose in the world? its duration?

12 ‣ When you have trouble staying awake, remember that working with and on behalf of others is in keeping with the laws of human nature and of your own constitution, whereas sleep is something you share with the brute beasts. Now, whatever is in keeping with a creature's own peculiar nature is more proper, and more fitting, and also more congenial.

13 ‣ Test every thought and sense perception, if possible, by the methods of science, the laws of morality, and the rules of logic.

14 ‣ Whenever you meet someone, ask yourself straightaway: What are the things that this person deems good and evil? For if he holds certain beliefs about pleasure and pain and the causes of each, about fame and obscurity, or about death and life, then I won't think it surprising or weird if he behaves in a certain way. Indeed, I'll regard it as inevitable.

15 ‣ Are you surprised to find a fig tree bearing figs? Then why wonder at the world when it bears its own peculiar crop of events? What an absurd contradiction! What kind of doctor or sea captain is surprised to find his patient with a fever or a contrary wind blowing?

16 ' Remember that you don't lose any freedom by changing your mind and accepting the correction of someone who points out your error. After all, it's your initiative, your judgment, indeed your intelligence that makes change and acceptance possible.

> REMEMBER THAT YOU DON'T LOSE ANY FREEDOM BY CHANGING YOUR MIND AND ACCEPTING THE CORRECTION OF SOMEONE WHO POINTS OUT YOUR ERROR.

17 ' If the decision rests with you, why do it? If with another, who's really to blame? The gods? The atoms? To blame either is pointless. Blame no one. If you can, correct the offender; if you can't, correct his offense; and if not even that's possible, what's the point in looking for someone to blame? Nothing should be done pointlessly.

18 ' What dies doesn't fall out of the universe. Here it stays, and here too it changes and dissolves into its primal elements, the same elements that make up the universe and you. These elements also change and murmur not.

19 ' Everything—horse, vine, anything—exists for a purpose. Is it any wonder? Even Helios the sun-god will say, "I have a job to do," and the rest of the gods will say the same. So what will you say? "I'm here to have a good time?" The very thought is beneath contempt.

20 ' Nature is as careful in planning the end of a thing as its beginning and middle. Consider the act of throwing a ball in the air. How does it benefit the ball to rise, or harm it to fall, or to come to rest on the ground? How is a bubble better for having been blown or worse for having burst? Likewise for a lamp.

21 ' Strip the body naked and see it for what it is, for what it becomes with age, disease, and debauchery. Short are the lives of

those who praise and of those who are praised, of those who remember and of those who are remembered. And even these lives are lived in but one small corner of this continent where men are not at peace with one another or with themselves—and the whole earth is the merest speck in space.

22 ᛫ Attend to the matter at hand, whether it be an object, an action, a moral principle, or the meaning of what is being said. You get what you deserve because you would rather *become* good tomorrow than *do* good today.

23 ᛫ Am I doing something? I do it for the good of mankind. Is something done to me? I accept it, referring it to the gods and to the source from which all things flow interdependently.

24 ᛫ Think of your bath—oil, sweat, grime, filthy water, all utterly disgusting. Such is every part of life and every material thing you treasure.

25 ᛫ Lucilla buried Verus, then Lucilla perished. Secunda and Maximus, Epitynchanus and Diotimus, Faustina and Antoninus, always the same story: Celer buries Hadrian, then it's Celer's turn. All those keen minds and noble natures of the past, some far-sighted, others puffed with their own importance, where are they now? Such brilliant wits as Charax, for instance, or Demetrius the Platonist and Eudaemon and others like them? All lasted for a day and are long dead—some no sooner dead than forgotten, others turned into legend and their legends already fading into oblivion. These should serve to remind you that your atoms will soon be scattered, or your breath simply snuffed out, or your component parts transmuted and placed into service somewhere else.

26 ᛫ Happy is the man who does the work of a man. And what is a man's work? To love his neighbor, to distrust the evidence of his senses, to distinguish false ideas from true, and to contemplate the works of nature.

27 ⸠ You have three relationships: the first is with your physical abode, the body; the second is with the divine source of everything; and the third is with those who share this life with you.

28 ⸠ Pain is either bad for the body (and if so, let the body say so) or for the soul. But the mind can refuse to regard pain as bad and thereby ensure the soul's unclouded calm and perfect equanimity. Every judgment of this sort, every impulse to act, every desire and aversion comes from within; nothing bad can gain entrance without the mind's consent.

29 ⸠ Erase false and fearful fancies by repeating to yourself: "No evil, no desire, no disturbance of any sort can gain entrance to my soul except I let them. By seeing things for what they are, I can use them for what they're worth." Remember that nature has planted this power in you.

30 ⸠ Whether speaking to the Senate or to the humblest person, use language that is respectful, but not affected. Let your speech be plain and honest.

31 ⸠ Look at the court of Augustus: his wife, daughter, children, ancestors, sister, Agrippa, relatives, members of his household, friends, Areius, Maecenas, his doctors, and priests—the entire court now dead. Then consider the deaths of others, not just the deaths of single individuals, but the extinction of whole lines, like the Pompeys. Think of the phrase inscribed on so many tombs: LAST OF HIS LINE. Imagine all the efforts his ancestors made to leave an heir, but in the end someone had to be last, and another line vanished from the earth.

32 ⸠ Build your life one action at a time, and be happy if each act you perform contributes to a fulfilling and complete life. No one can prevent you from doing this.

"But what if some outside circumstance stands in my way?"

Not even that can stop you from acting justly, wisely, and reasonably.

"But it may block me from doing something I want to do."

Yes, but by welcoming the obstacle and by calmly adapting your action to it, you will be able to do something else in harmony with your goals and with the sort of life you are seeking to build.

33 · Modest in victory; graceful in defeat.

34 · Have you ever seen a hand or foot cut off, or a head severed and lying apart from the rest of the body? This is exactly what a man does to himself, so far as he is able, when he refuses to accept what happens and distances himself from others or behaves churlishly. You are torn from the unity of nature into which you were born a part and from which you have now cut yourself off.

But here's an astounding thought: you are still capable of rejoining that unity! To no other part of his creation has God granted the power to rejoin the whole once it has been cut off or severed. Notice with what generosity God has dignified man. Not only has God given him the power to remain united with the whole, but if man cuts himself off from the whole, he has provided the means for him to rejoin the whole and play his part again.

35 · Nature equips rational beings with the same powers as herself. Just as nature works on whatever opposes or resists her, giving it a place in the necessary order and making it part of herself, so too can a rational being convert every hindrance into material for himself and use it for his own ends.

36 · Don't panic before the picture of your entire life. Don't dwell on all the troubles you've faced or have yet to face, but instead ask yourself as each trouble comes: What is so unbearable or unmanageable in this? Your reply will embarrass you. Then remind yourself that it's not the future or the past that bears down on you, but only the present, always the present, which becomes an even smaller thing when isolated in this way and when the mind that cannot bear up under so slender an object is chastened.

37 · Does Pantheia or Pergamus still sit in mourning by the tomb of Verus? Is Chabrias or Diotimus weeping at Hadrian's grave? Ridicu-

lous! And if they were, would the dead feel their presence? And if they did, would they be pleased? And if pleased, would their pleasure make the mourners immortal? Are the mourners not fated like those they mourn to become old women and old men, and then to die? And what would be left for the dead to do after the mourners died? This is all stench and gore in a sack!

38 ‣ If you have a sharp eye, says the proverb, then look sharp, seeing the right course and judging wisely.

39 ‣ In the make-up of a rational being, I can see no virtue incompatible with justice, but I do find a virtue at odds with pleasure: self-control.

40 ‣ If you give up your opinion about what appears to cause you pain, then you cannot be harmed. "Who is the you that does this?" Your reason. "But reason and I are not the same." So be it. Then let your reason not be harmed, and if any other part of you appears to feel pain, let it form its own opinion and keep that to itself.

41 ‣ Any hindrance to the senses is a bad thing for our animal nature, as is any obstacle to desire. There are also obstructions harmful to the nature of plants. Similarly, any impediment to clear thinking is bad for an intelligent nature. Now apply all this to yourself. Are you affected by pain or pleasure? Let the senses handle that. Are you thwarted in the achievement of a goal or desire? If you desired without restraint or reservation, you violated your intelligent nature. Desire instead within the limits imposed by reason, and all obstacles and injuries will disappear. Nothing can rule or impede the mind within its own kingdom—neither fire nor sword, not a tyrant or slander, nothing whatsoever. "The perfect sphere, once spun and true, remains spherical."

42 ‣ Since I've never intentionally harmed another, what right have I to injure myself?

43 ‣ Some delight in this; others in that. My delight is in clear thinking and a clean conscience, in not turning away from any man or

from anything that happens to men, but in looking on all with compassion and using everything according to its worth.

44 · Give yourself the present. Those who chase after future fame fail to realize that the men whose praise they crave tomorrow will be no different from the men whose opinions they despise today, and all these men will die. What do you care whether tomorrow's men know the sound of your name or say nice things about you?

45 · Take and toss me wherever you want. My soul will remain invincible and at peace, content to be and to act in harmony with its own rules. Is a mere change of scene capable of disturbing or debasing my soul, causing it to crave or cower, sink or quake? What could possibly cause this?!

46 · Nothing can happen to a man that isn't natural to men. Likewise, what happens to cattle, vines, and stones is natural to each. What is there to complain about when all these things endure only what is usual and natural? Nature allows nothing that you can't handle.

47 · If you're troubled by something outside yourself, it isn't the thing itself that bothers you, but your opinion of it, and this opinion you have the power to revoke immediately. If what troubles you arises from some flaw in your character or disposition, who prevents you from correcting the flaw? If it's your failure to do some good or necessary work that frustrates you, why not put your energy into doing it rather than fretting about it?

"But something stronger than I prevents me."

Then don't worry. It isn't your responsibility to do what you lack the power to do.

"But if it isn't done, life isn't worth living."

Then quit this

> IF YOU'RE TROUBLED BY SOMETHING OUTSIDE YOURSELF, IT ISN'T THE THING ITSELF THAT BOTHERS YOU, BUT YOUR OPINION OF IT, AND THIS OPINION YOU HAVE THE POWER TO REVOKE IMMEDIATELY.

life in peace, as one who dies full of good works and forgiveness for those who opposed him.

48 ' You will recall how impregnable your mind is when it withdraws into itself and steadfastly refuses to do what it doesn't want to do, even when its refusal is unreasonable. Imagine then what it's like when it arrives at a decision calmly and reasonably. Free from passions, the mind is a veritable fortress. A man cannot find a more secure place to take refuge and remain unassailable forever. Ignorant is he who fails to see this, and truly ill-fated is he who sees but fails to take refuge.

49 ' Don't make more of things than what your senses initially tell you. You are told, for example, that someone has been gossiping about you. Okay, but you *aren't* told that this chatter hurt you. Or you may see your child is sick. Yes, but you *don't* see he's in danger. Always stick to your first impressions, and don't begin adding inferences of your own, and you'll be safe. Or rather add this observation only: everything that happens is part of the natural and familiar order of things.

50 ' "The cucumber is bitter." Throw it away. "There's a briar in my path." Walk around it. That's enough. Don't feel compelled to add, "Why are these things allowed to happen?" The naturalist will only have a good laugh at your expense, as would the carpenter or shoemaker if you complained about sawdust or leather trimmings in their workshops. Still, these craftsmen have a place to throw their debris, whereas nature has no such place, yet the wonder of her craft is that she is able, without going outside herself, to transform what appears worn out, old, and useless into entirely new creations. She uses no materials outside herself and has no need of a scrap heap. She labors contentedly in her own space, with her own materials, at her own art.

BOOK NINE

1 · He sins who acts unjustly. All rational creatures, by nature's deep design and purpose, are created for one another. They are meant to help those who deserve help and in no way to harm one another. He who shrugs off the will of nature sins against the oldest of the gods.

He who tells lies sins against the same god. Nature is the basis for everything that is, and everything that is is intimately connected with everything that ever was. Truth is just another name for nature, the first cause of everything. He who lies with the intent of deceiving another sins by acting unjustly, but he who lies unintentionally sins by striking a discordant note with nature and by opposing the profound harmony of the universe. By opposing the truth, even unwittingly, the liar declares war on nature and loses through neglect his god-given ability to discern what is true and what is false.

He also sins who pursues pleasures as if they were good and flees hardships as if they were evil. Seeing how often evildoers enjoy pleasures and acquire things that bring pleasure while decent folk suffer hardships and encounter things that cause pain, this sort of person cannot help but blame nature for handing out pleasures and hardships indiscriminately. Moreover, the person afraid of hardship is at odds with something that is going to happen as part of the natural order of things, and this is sinful. Likewise, the person panting after pleasure will not hesitate to act unjustly, and this is clearly sinful.

Nature would not provide for both pleasures and hardships were she not indifferent to both, and those who would follow nature and be of one mind with her must be indifferent when she is indifferent. Whoever then fails to follow nature by being indifferent to hardship and pleasure, death and life, obscurity and fame, that person obviously offends the gods.

Now, by saying that nature uses these things indifferently, I mean that all things follow from one another in a sequence begun by the original impulse of Providence and continued in accordance with certain ordering principles and generative powers such as matter, change, and succession.

2 · It would be best never to have tasted deceit, hypocrisy, luxury, and pride; but the next best course would be, despising these things, to push away from the table. Do you choose instead to persist in these evils? Has experience not convinced you to flee this plague? Is not the corruption of your mind and soul a plague far more deadly than any pollution or contamination in the air you breathe? This plague attacks us only as animals, but that destroys our humanity.

3 · Don't fear death, but give it a friendly greeting. Nature sends it along with everything else. Like youth and old age, growing up and reaching one's prime, growing teeth and a beard and white hair, begetting and conceiving and bearing children—our dissolution is just one of life's natural processes. A man who has given it any thought will never approach death carelessly, hastily, or scornfully, but he will wait for it as he would for any natural process. As you now wait for the unborn child to burst from your wife's womb, so should you anticipate the moment when your soul will slip from its shell.

But if your trembling heart needs a cruder form of reassurance, consider the worth of the material objects you're leaving behind and the morals of those with whom you'll no longer have to associate. Although it's your job to treat them gently and compassionately, and not to criticize them, it's fair to bear in mind that you're not parting from like-minded men. This alone, if nothing else, could drag you back from the brink of death and force you to go on living: the company of kindred spirits. But as it is, so great is the weariness of living in discord with your fellow men that you say, "Come quickly, Death, lest I, like them, forget myself."

4 · The sinner sins against himself. The unjust man does injustice to himself by making himself bad.

5 · Injustice results as often from not doing as from doing.

6 · It is enough when you are thinking objectively, behaving courteously, and feeling easy about circumstances outside your control.

7 · Blot out imagination; restrain impulse; stifle desire; give your reason the upper hand.

8 · One vital spirit is distributed among the animals, and one rational spirit is allotted to mankind. There is also one earth for all creatures that live on the earth and share a single light by which they see and a single atmosphere by which they breath.

9 · Things that share a common element or characteristic are naturally drawn to one another. Earthy objects gravitate toward the earth, and fluids tend to flow together, as do gases, so that only barriers and force can keep them apart. Fire leaps toward the sun, the elemental fire, and is so eager to join other fires that objects with the least dryness—lacking the ingredients necessary to resist—will enable it to break out. In the same way, those who share the one rational spirit are eager to join their own kind, nay, even more eager, since the tendency to mix and mingle with their own kind is in proportion to their superiority over other things.

Note, for example, that in animals without reason we find bees in swarms, cattle in herds, birds in flocks, and similar "love groupings." The vital spirit present in these makes the grouping tendency much stronger than it is in plants or rocks or trees. And in rational creatures we see cities and friendships, families and assemblies, while in wartime there are treaties and truces. And in the case of superior things like stars, we discover a kind of unity in separation. The higher we rise on the scale of being, the easier it is to discern a connection even among things separated by vast distances.

Look at what happens now. Only rational creatures now forget their attraction to one another; only among them do we fail to see conver-

> YOU'RE MORE LIKELY TO FIND
> A CLOD OF EARTH
> DETACHED FROM THE EARTH
> THAN A MAN ENTIRELY
> CUT OFF FROM MANKIND.

gence and agreement. But even as they flee from one another, they keep running into themselves, for nature is too strong for them. Pay close attention, and you'll see what I mean. You're more likely to find a clod of earth detached from the earth than a man entirely cut off from mankind.

10 ' Everything bears fruit—Man, God, the Universe—each in its own season. It doesn't matter that this manner of speaking is customarily reserved for the vine and other plants. Reason also bears fruit, both for itself and for everything else, and all its fruit tastes of sweet reasonableness.

11 ' If you can, change their evil ways by teaching them. If that doesn't work, remember that kindness is a virtue you possess for this very situation. The gods themselves are kind to such men and sometimes even assist them in their efforts to become healthy or wealthy or famous. You can do the same. What's stopping you?

12 ' Work hard, not like a slave who looks for pity or praise, but as one who strives single-mindedly to discharge his social obligations.

13 ' Today, I got out of trouble, or rather I got trouble out of me. The trouble was not outside, but inside, and depended on my point of view.

14 ' Everything's the same: experience is banal, time is fleeting, and matter is corrupt. It's just what it was in the days of those we've buried.

15 ' Outside the door lies the world of things, a world unto itself. Things have no knowledge of themselves, nor can they speak for themselves. What can know and speak for them? The discerning mind.

16 ' Good and evil lie in a rational and social being's deeds, not in his feelings. Likewise, virtue and vice are terms applied to deeds, not feelings.

17 · To a stone thrown up in the air, there is no evil in falling or good in rising.

18 · Delve into what motivates and governs them, and you will expose the critics you fear and see what poor critics they are of themselves.

19 · All is change. You yourself are continuously changing and being destroyed bit by bit. So is the whole universe.

20 · Another's wrongdoing—leave it alone.

21 · The conclusion of an activity, the end or what might be called the death of an impulse or opinion, there's no evil in these. Look at the various stages of life, childhood, boyhood, manhood, old age; each ended in a kind of death. Was it so dreadful? Think now about the life you lived with your grandfather, then with your mother, then with your father. Looking at these and all the other changes, transformations, and endings that have happened in your life, ask yourself, "Was there anything to be feared in all this?" No, no more than in the end, the cessation, the transformation of life itself.

22 · Make haste to examine your own mind, the mind of the universe, and the mind of your neighbor. Your own mind to make sure it is just. The mind of the universe to remind yourself of what you are a part. Your neighbor's mind to figure out whether he acted knowingly or out of ignorance, and while doing this to reflect that he is your brother.

23 · Just as you are part of the whole community, each of your actions should contribute to the whole life of the community. Any action of yours that fails, directly or remotely, to make this contribution, fragments the life of the community and jeopardizes its unity. It's a rebellious act, like the man in a town meeting who holds himself aloof and refuses to come to any agreement with his neighbors.

24 • Children's temper tantrums, games of make believe, and "little breaths sustaining corpses"—Homer's underworld is more solid than this!

25 • Get at the underlying cause of a thing, and study it apart from its material effects. Then determine how long this type of cause can sustain its effects.

26 • You have suffered a thousand ills because you are not content to be ruled by reason, as nature intended. Stop! Enough!

27 • When men hate or blame you, or say hurtful things about you, look deeply into their hearts and see what kind of men they are. You'll see how unnecessary it is to strain after their good opinion. Yet you must still think kindly of them. They are your neighbors. The gods help them as they do you, by dreams and oracles, to win their hearts' desires.

28 • Up and down, from age to age, the world's repeating cycles are the same. Either the cosmic mind initiates everything individually (in which case welcome whatever it initiates), or else it initiated things once for all time and every subsequent effect serves also as a cause. Destiny or atoms, what does it matter? If God is discharging every detail, then all is well; and if everything's a matter of chance, still you don't have to be ruled by chance.

The earth will soon cover us all. Then the earth itself will change, and that changed earth will change again, and then again, changing into eternity. Anyone who contemplates these endless waves of change and transformation will look with indifference on every mortal thing.

29 • The cosmic cause is an onrushing flood that carries all before it. How piddling are these little men who play the statesmen and imagine they act like philosophers! Drooling toddlers! What does it take to be a man? Do what nature demands at this moment. Just do it, if you can, and don't be looking around to see if someone is watching. Don't look for Plato's Republic either. Be content if you can take

a small step, and know that even this is no mean feat. For you're not going to change their hearts, and failing that, all is pretense. Only slavish obedience and whining submission are possible. Go ahead and tell me about Alexander, Philip, or Demetrius of Phalerum. If they were schooled by nature, that's their business. But if they merely acted the part of tragic heroes, no one has condemned me to follow their lead. Simplicity and modesty are the fruits of philosophy; keep me from becoming pompous and proud.

30 · Look down from the sky at all the herds of men, their countless ceremonies, their endless voyages to and fro in both calm and storm, and the amazing diversity of creatures that are born, make a life with one another, and disappear. Imagine the life of those who lived long ago, or the life of those who will live after you are dead, or the life now being lived in distant foreign lands. How many don't even know your name? How many who do will soon forget it? How many who praise you today will slander you tomorrow? Memory, fame, and the like—all counterfeit.

31 · When facing whatever happens outside your control, be calm; when taking actions for which you are responsible, be fair. In other words, whether acting or reacting, your aim is the aid and betterment of others, in fulfillment of nature's laws.

> WHEN FACING WHATEVER
> HAPPENS OUTSIDE YOUR CONTROL,
> BE CALM; WHEN TAKING ACTIONS
> FOR WHICH YOU ARE RESPONSIBLE,
> BE FAIR.

32 · Many of the things that trouble you are easily disposed of, for they are all in your mind. Instead of dwelling on them in such cramped quarters, why not inhabit spacious chambers by taking into your mind the whole wide world, the vast expanse of eternity, the swift succession of change in the smallest parts of everything. How short is the span between birth and death, how bottomless the abyss before birth and boundless the gulf after death.

33 ⋅ What you now see will soon perish, and those who watch it perish will pass away themselves no less quickly. The man who outlives all his friends will join the friend he lost as a boy in the grave.

34 ⋅ Examine their guiding principles. What sorts of things do they go after? What sorts of people inspire their love and admiration? Cast a cold eye on their naked little souls. These are the same who think that their jeers sting or their cheers warm? What presumption!

35 ⋅ Loss and change: two words for the same thing. Nature rejoices in change. Through her all things come into being and are arranged in the same way as they were in the beginning and will be to the end. How then can you say that everything is coming out badly and is bound to come out badly in the end? How then can you say that not all the gods in heaven have the power to set things right? How then can you say that an ill wind is fated to blow through the world forever?

36 ⋅ The decay at the core of everything renders water, dust, bones, stench. Marble is simply age-hardened slabs of earth; gold and silver, sediments of earth; fine clothing, the hair of animals; purple dye, the blood of fish; and so on. Our very breath is the same, constantly passing from one lung to the next.

37 ⋅ Enough of this pathetic way of life, this continual complaining and aping of others. Why worry? There's nothing new for you to get all worked up about. Do the causes of things disturb you? Then look to them. Or is it the things themselves? Then take a hard look at them. Formal cause and material effect—that's all there is. What matters at this late date is to be simpler and better in the eyes of God. This is so whether you ponder the meaning of life for three hundred years or three.

38 ⋅ If he did wrong, then he harms himself. And what if he did no wrong?

39 ⋅ Either everything springs from a single intelligent source that rules it as the mind does the body, in which case no part should com-

plain about what is organized for the good of the whole, or everything is made up of atoms, randomly mixing and dispersing. So why do you worry? Say to your true, independent, and governing self: "You're dead. You're a rotting corpse. You've decided to become an actor and play a wild beast running with the herd. Well then, eat grass."

40 ⬝ Either the gods are powerful or they are powerless. If they are powerless, why bother praying? But if they are powerful, why not ask them to free you from the fear or desire or sorrow caused by something, rather than asking them to give or withhold the thing itself? If the gods help men at all, this is surely the way they do it.

But you might object, "The gods have left these things up to me."

Well, if that is the case, is it not better to use freely what is left up to you than to beg slavishly for what is out of your hands? Who told you that the gods do not also help us with the things they leave up to us? Begin to pray this way, and see what happens:

One man prays, "Help me seduce this woman," but you pray instead, "Prevent me from lusting after her."

Another prays, "Rid me of my enemy," but you pray, "Rid me of the desire to be rid of my enemy."

Another, "Do not take my dear child from me," but you, "May I not fear the loss of my child."

Turn your prayers in this direction, and see what comes of it.

41 ⬝ "During my illnesses," says Epicurus, "I never talked about my aches and pains, or bothered those who came to see me with such trifles. Rather I continued to discuss the fundamental principles of science, in particular how the mind, while fully aware of all the body's movements, remains unmoved and attends to its own good. Nor did I submit to the doctors," he continues, "and give them a chance to boast of their medical expertise and make a fuss over me, but I just lived my life in good health and spirits."

Whether in sickness, if you are sick, or in any other circumstance, be like Epicurus. Let no difficulty or hardship cause you to abandon philosophy or to tune in to the gossip of the foolish and uneducated. (On this piece of advice, all schools of philosophy are agreed.) Keep to the task at hand, and to the tool you possess for completing it.

42 ' Whenever somebody's shameless behavior offends you, immediately ask yourself: "Can there be a world without shameless people in it?" Of course not. Don't demand the impossible. This is just another one of those shameless people whom the world cannot be without. Keep the same question handy for scoundrels, cheaters, and other kinds of wrongdoers. By bearing in mind that there are bound to be people like this, you will find individuals like this easier to endure.

At the same time ask yourself: "What virtue has nature given me to cope with this vice?" The antibody against loutish behavior, for example, is gentleness. Against every vice there is a power to combat it, and broadly speaking, you have the power to help any man find his way. The wrongdoer is, after all, merely missing his true mark and has lost his way. Besides, how has he harmed you? None of those with whom you're upset has done a thing to impair your ability to think, and no evil or harm can come to you except your thinking let it.

What's so bad or surprising about the ignoramus who acts out of ignorance? Find fault instead with yourself for failing to anticipate his offensive behavior. Your ability to reason should have told you that he would misbehave, but you refused to listen and are now shocked by his misbehavior.

Indeed, whenever you feel inclined to blame someone for deceit or ingratitude, turn the accusation upon yourself. Obviously, the fault lies with you if you trusted a liar to keep his word, or if you did a good deed with some string attached and without expecting the doing of the deed to be its own reward.

Having done a good deed, what more do you want? Isn't it enough to have acted in harmony with your nature? Do you need to be paid for it as well? Do the eyes demand payment for seeing, or the feet wages for walking? Just as these organs were made for what they do and find fulfillment in doing what they were made to do, so too are men made by nature for one another. Whenever they perform a good deed or contribute to the common good in some way, they do what they were made to do and receive all that is theirs.

BOOK TEN

1 · Is it possible that one day I shall see you, O my soul, good, simple, indivisible, stripped of every pretense, more solid than the flesh that now covers you? Will you ever know a day of unclouded love and tenderness? Will you ever be content—no hopes, no regrets, needing nothing, desiring nothing, animate or inanimate, not even for a moment's pleasure—nor wanting a little more time to prolong the ecstasy, or a more pleasing room or view or climate, or more sweet accord in your relations with others? When will you be content with your present condition, happy with all you have, accepting it as a gift from the gods and acknowledging that all is well with you and that all will be well? When will you understand that the gods hold dear those gifts (the good, the just, the beautiful) they intend for the preservation of a perfect living whole—gifts that nourish the universe by gathering and binding the primal elements dispersed by dissolution and decay and needed for each new creation? Will there ever come a day, O my soul, when you can live in the company of men and gods, blameless in their eyes, without blaming them at all?

2 · Since you are governed by inanimate nature, pay attention to what it is telling you and act upon it, unless your animal nature objects. In that case, obey your animal nature without hesitation, unless it is contradicted in turn by reason. (The dictates of reason, of course, also cover the norms of society.) Apply these rules to your life, and get on with it.

3 · Whatever happens, either you have the strength to bear it or you don't. If you have the strength, stop complaining, be grateful, and bear it. If you lack the strength, there is still no reason to lose patience, for once your strength is consumed, the struggle will end. But remember, you have the power within you to endure anything,

for your mere opinion can render it tolerable, perhaps even acceptable, by regarding it as an opportunity for enlightenment or a matter of duty.

4 ⸱ If someone makes a mistake, correct him with kindness and point out where he went wrong. If you fail, blame only yourself, or better yet, don't blame anyone.

5 ⸱ Whatever happens to you was destined to happen from before time began. Your entire existence as well as the smallest details of your works and days were woven into the woof of cause, the weft of effect from all eternity.

6 ⸱ Whether the universe is composed of an infinite number of blind atoms or one all-seeing nature, two things are clear: first, I am a part of the universe governed by nature; and second, I am related in some way to the other parts like myself. Once I acknowledge this, I shall be content with any role the universe assigns me, for nothing is bad for the part that is good for the whole, and the whole contains nothing which is not good for it. This is true for everything in nature, but the world has an additional safeguard: nothing from outside can interfere or force it to generate something harmful to itself.

Realizing that I am part of just such a universe, I will calmly accept whatever happens. And because I am related to the other parts like myself, I will not seek my own advantage at their expense, but I will study to know what is our common good and bend every effort to advance that good and to dissuade others from acting against it. If I am successful in this, my life is bound to flow smoothly, as one would expect for the dutiful citizen who is always looking out for others and enjoys whatever work his community asks of him.

7 ⸱ It is necessary for everything in the universe to perish, which is the same as saying that all parts of the whole must change. Now if the atrophy and extinction of its parts are unintended, it is difficult to see how the whole universe can escape deterioration and eventual death.

Has nature chosen to damage its own parts by making them susceptible to harm and bent on harming one another, or did this happen without nature's knowledge and participation? Neither of these possibilities seems likely. Or suppose we leave a purposeful nature out of it and say that this is just the way things are? How absurd it then is in one breath to say that everything in the universe is bound to change and in the next breath to express shock or resentment at a particular change as though it were in violation of some moral or physical law, especially in light of the fact that each part tends to return to the primal elements from which it originated.

Consider this protean process. Either the atoms making up the parts are dispersed or what is solid returns to earth and what is gas rejoins the air in such a way that these elements re-enter the womb of being, which is either periodically consumed by fire or continually renewed by the return of its offspring. If you ascribe to the second theory, it would be a mistake to assume that your solid and gaseous parts date from birth. They are no older than the food you ate and the air you breathed yesterday or the day before. All of this change, therefore, works upon a part or, if you will, a person who is in a continual state of flux, constantly being re-created, and no longer the same baby his mother once bore. Nor do I see any contradiction in the fact that we identify this metamorphosing part or person as one and the same over time.

8 · When you allow others to call you good, modest, sincere, openminded, fair-minded, high-minded, be sure that you don't disappoint them, or if you do, be quick to restore these virtues to their eyes. Remember that the open-minded attend meticulously to details and work through problems without being distracted; that the fairminded accept gladly the conditions that nature imposes; that the high-minded place reason above the storms and doldrums of the flesh, that is, above fame, death, and the like.

In fact, if you can learn to embody these virtues rather than just to wear them for appearances' sake, you will be a new man, and you will begin to live a new life. To continue in your old life, perpetually distracted by something or disgruntled with someone, shows no more intelligence and courage than gladiators who, half devoured by wild beasts, their bodies gaping with wounds and drenched in gore, beg to be kept alive for one more day when all they have to look forward to is facing again the same claws and fangs.

Cast off with these few faithful friends, and know that if you sail in close company with them, they will surely bring you to the Isles of the Blessed. But if you find yourself unable to keep up and falling behind, be a man and make a decent life in some quiet corner of the world, or failing that, take leave of this life altogether, not in a foul temper, but simply, freely, honorably, having succeeded at least in making a brave end.

This afterthought: Lest you become distracted with the titles others give you and the noble attributes they ascribe to you, you should bear in mind that the gods themselves are not interested in this sort of flattery. They desire instead for all rational beings to imitate their attributes for the purpose of becoming like them, just as the fig tree does the work of a fig tree, the dog the work of a dog, the bee the work of a bee, and man the work of a man.

9 ، Hysteria, combat, terror, lethargy, servility, the stuff of daily existence—these attenuate the sacred principles which, unless rooted deep in a reflective life, are easily discarded. Let this be your goal: in all things to act with dispatch while making thorough observations, taking into consideration any relevant theories, and preserving your knowledge of the most minute and concrete details. When will you learn to seek your happiness in the simple things, in dignity, in the knowledge of what is at the heart of each thing, its place in the world, its length of days, its composition, to whom it belongs, and whose it is to give or take away?

10 ، A spider glories in trapping a fly—so does one man in catching a hare, another in netting a sardine, another boars, or bears, or Sarmatians? Examine their principles. Are they not all thieves and cutthroats?

11 ، Develop your own methods for observing how all things are in a continual state of change, one into another. Be ready, and welcome it when it is your turn to experience change, for there is nothing like it to heighten your sensibilities and elevate your mind. At the moment

of change, a man's soul takes flight, and being in this instant reminded that he will soon be called upon to leave the world of things and the company of men, he devotes himself wholeheartedly to justice in whatever he does and to nature in whatever is done to him. His mind is no longer troubled by what someone may say or think about him, or do against him; and he finds perfect contentment in these two things only: to do the task at hand justly and to embrace his fate gladly.

Throwing off all other considerations and schemes, his one ambition is to run the straight race marked out by the law, in pursuit of the swift-footed gods, who never leave this sure course.

> BE READY, AND WELCOME IT WHEN IT IS YOUR TURN TO EXPERIENCE CHANGE, FOR THERE IS NOTHING LIKE IT TO HEIGHTEN YOUR SENSIBILITIES AND ELEVATE YOUR MIND.

12 ∙ Why do you hesitate or second-guess yourself when you know perfectly well what ought to be done? If you know where you need to go, make a considerate but determined effort to get there. If you don't, wait and seek the best advice you can find. If you meet with resistance along the way, advance cautiously and prepare at any moment to take refuge in what you know to be just, for to reach your goal justly is the apotheosis of achievement whereas to advance even one inch by doing an injustice is the most miserable form of failure. Relaxed but alert, cheerful but determined—such is reason's faithful follower.

13 ∙ From the moment you wake up, ask yourself: Does it really matter if someone criticizes my correct and just acts? Not at all. How can you forget how those who take pride in praising and blaming others behave in bed and at table—what they pursue, what they flee, what they lust after, what they reveal, what they snatch and make away with, not with their hands and feet, but with the noblest part of themselves, the very part from which springs, if they will it, faith, honor, truth, loyalty, and a good spirit.

14 ' To nature, the giver and taker of all things, the wise and self-respecting man says, "Give what it is your pleasure to give; take what you will." This he says, not in a tone of swaggering machismo, but in an attentive and obedient voice.

15 ' What remains of life is short. Live it as if on craggy mountain heights, for what does it matter where one lives? Whether in a city or in the wilderness, you are a citizen of the world. Let men behold in you a true man, one who lives in harmony with nature. If they can't bear it, let them put you to death. Better to die than to live like them.

> STOP ALL THIS THEORIZING
> ABOUT WHAT A GOOD MAN
> SHOULD BE. BE IT!

16 ' Stop all this theorizing about what a good man should be. Be it!

17 ' Strive continually to imagine time eternal and space infinite. Then tell yourself that a planet in space is but a fig seed; an epoch in time like the twist of a tendril.

18 ' Focus on any material object. See how it is changing before your eyes—dissolving, decaying, dissipating—and in what way it is born to die.

19 ' Eating, sleeping, copulating, defecating—just look at them! See what airs they put on, becoming puffed up or lapsing into paroxysms of rage, overwhelming us with their high-sounding reproaches! It wasn't long ago they were toadies sucking up to some boss, and it won't be long before they're groveling again.

20 ' What nature gives is best, and best too at the time it is given.

21 ' "The earth loves rain, and holy ether too . . ." Yes, how nature loves to create whatever is to be! To this nature I profess, "I share your love." Is this not what we mean when we say, "Love will find a way"?

22 ⸱ Either you go on living here at the center of things; or you withdraw from the active life and move away; or you die and your work is done. There's no other choice but these—so take heart!

23 ⸱ Bear in mind that your hermitage goes wherever you go. The good life is the same here as it is in the mountains or by the sea. It is as Plato said, ". . . sheltered in his mountain fold, milking his bleating flocks."

24 ⸱ What is this governing self I'm supposed to have? Of what use is it? Is it serving some purpose at this moment? Can it reason? Is it severed from society and incapable of forming human attachments? Has it so melted into my flesh and melded with my body that it is no longer free?

25 ⸱ The slave who flees his master is a runaway. The law too is a master, and whoever breaks it is in the same position as the runaway slave. Likewise, those who become irritable, angry, or afraid because something has already happened, is just happening, or is about to happen are, in effect, refusing to accept the natural and causal laws of the universe. In giving way to irritation, anger, or fear, they are no better than runaway slaves.

26 ⸱ A man ejaculates into a womb and goes about his business, and some time later a new cause discovers his sperm, works on it, and produces a fully formed baby. What an astonishing sequence of events! Later this baby begins to swallow food that disappears down its throat where another cause takes over to produce sensation and emotion, in a word, life and vital energy in all its forms. Contemplate these mysteries and observe their hidden power which can be seen just as clearly as the uplifting and downpressing force of gravity, although not with the eyes.

27 ⸱ Keep in mind that what goes on today went on yesterday and will go on again tomorrow. From your own experience or from your reading of history, you have taken in the same shows, watched the very same scenes staged by the court of Hadrian, the court of Anton-

inus, and the courts of Philip, Alexander, Croesus. Same shows, same scenes, same parts. Only the names of the actors change.

28 ' The next time you hear someone bemoaning his fate or complaining about something, visualize the pig at a sacrifice, squealing and kicking. It's the same with the person who lies upon his lonely bed, lamenting his pains or cursing his constraints in silence. Only the rational being can embrace his fate and follow the course of events willingly; those who howl and whine can merely follow.

29 ' Every time you do something, stop and ask yourself: "Is death to be feared because it will deprive me of this?"

30 ' Whenever you are about to find fault with someone, ask yourself the following question: What fault of mine most nearly resembles the one I am about to criticize? Is it love of money? or pleasure? or reputation? and so on until you have identified the closest cousin. By redirecting your attention in this way, you will soon forget your anger as you realize that he can't help himself any more than you can. How can he possibly overcome the compulsion to do wrong? If you can help him with this, you have helped yourself as well.

31 ' When you see Satyron, imagine someone long dead like Socraticus, Eutyches, or Hymen. When it is Euphrates you are looking at, think of him as Eutychion or Silvanus. For Alciphron, substitute Tropaiophoros; and seeing Severus, imagine Crito or Xenophon. When you look at yourself, think of one of the Caesars of old, and similarly with everyone, make this substitution and ask yourself, "Where are they all now?" Nowhere, or nobody knows where. This habit will help you see all things human as smoke and nothingness, especially if you remember that once a thing changes it ceases to exist for all eternity.

Why then get all wound up? Why not be content to pass your short time here in an orderly way? What material condition or station in life can you possibly be afraid of, since everything gives you an opportunity to exercise your reason in making an accurate and philosophical assessment of life? Persevere, then, until you have learned everything life has to teach you, the way a healthy stomach digests all sorts of food and a roaring fire converts whatever is heaped on it to heat and light.

32 ˙ Let no one be able to say truthfully that you are not honest or good. If someone says this, you have the power to make him a liar. Who prevents you from being honest and good? You need only resolve to end your life if you cannot be such a man, for in this case not even reason obliges you to go on living.

33 ˙ What is the very best you can say or do with the material you have to work with? Whatever that is, you can say or do it. Make no excuse by claiming that something prevents you.

You will never stop bemoaning your fate until it becomes as natural for you to follow the law of your being—in whatever material conditions you find yourself—as it is for a hedonist to go after pleasure. Indeed, every opportunity to speak or act according to the law of your being should give you pleasure, and that opportunity exists everywhere.

A cylinder is not free to roll at will, nor is fire or water or anything else that is governed by the nature peculiar to souls without reason. Many hindrances and obstacles stand in their way. Intelligence and reason, on the other hand, possess both the nature and the will to surmount obstacles in their path. See how reason overcomes whatever hinders it with the ease of fire rising, a stone dropping, or a cylinder rolling down a slope. Look no farther than this.

The remaining obstacles either act upon the body, an inanimate object, or they are powerless to defeat or do harm unless the mind yield to a false impression or surrender its own reason. Were this not so, these obstacles would have the effect of making a man bad. We observe the proof of this in nature. Whenever anything is hindered, its condition deteriorates and becomes worse, whereas a man actually becomes better and more praiseworthy when he overcomes what hinders him through the use of reason.

In summary, remember that whatever does not hurt the man who is by nature a citizen does not hurt the City, nor is the City hurt by what does not hurt the law. Now, not one of all the things a man is apt to call bad luck hurts the law; therefore, bad luck cannot hurt the City or the citizen either.

34 ⸱ For the man who feels the bite of truth, even the most succinct and commonplace saying helps guard him against grief and fear. This, for example:

> The generations of men—
> leaves the wind scatters
> over the face of the earth.

Your children are tender leaves as well. Leaves too are the crowd that wants you to hear their shouts of praise, or that curses you openly or blames and scoffs behind your back. Leaves likewise are those on whom the memory of your fame rests. For all these

> Blossom in the springtime

and are soon blown away by the autumn winds, and the forest replaces them all. A short life characterizes everything, yet you pursue or shun these things as if they held the secret of life everlasting. A little while and you will close your eyes, and not long after someone else will mourn the one who bore you to the grave.

35 ⸱ The healthy eye sees whatever is visible and does not say, like someone suffering from ophthalmia, "I want only to see what is green." Having a healthy sense of hearing and smell means being alert to every sound and scent. The healthy stomach can digest all kinds of food, like the molar that is prepared to grind whatever we put in our mouths. Just so, the healthy mind should be prepared for whatever happens. The mind protesting, "Keep my children from dying!" and "May all men praise every little thing I do!" is an eye looking only for what is green and a tooth wanting only what is easy to chew.

36 ⸱ No one is possessed of such good fortune that he can lie dying without being circled by people rejoicing at his imminent demise.

Was he high-minded and wise? Then you can be sure that someone will be muttering to himself, "Now we can breathe easy again with that schoolmaster out of the way. Although he was never harsh with any of us, I always felt he was silently judging us." So much for the virtuous man's reward. As for the rest of us, think of all the good reasons we have given our friends to be happy to be rid of us.

Think of this at the approach of death, and ease your passing with these reflections: "In the life I am leaving behind, even the friends for whom I toiled and prayed and agonized so much wanted me out of the way, hoping by my death to gain some sort of relief." Why then should you wish to lengthen your stay?

But do not because of this leave any less well disposed to them. Be true to your best self, friendly, good-natured, and kind. Leave them not as a man being torn away, but die a peaceful death with the soul slipping easily from the body. Nature brought you together and tied you to them, and now she cuts the knot. I am separated as from kins-men. I am not dragged away, and I do not resist. It is just another natural act.

> THINK OF ALL THE GOOD REASONS WE HAVE GIVEN OUR FRIENDS TO BE HAPPY TO BE RID OF US.

37 · In everything you see someone else do, make it a habit to ask yourself, "What is his purpose in doing this?" But begin with yourself. Question your own actions first.

38 · Remember, what pulls the strings is a power hidden deep within you: it is what moves you; it is life; it is—one might even say—the man himself. Never make the mistake of picturing it with the fleshy shell encasing it or the organs attached to it. These are like a carpenter's tools, except that they are joined to the body by nature. Without the inner power that moves or stays these parts, they are as useless as a weaver's shuttle, a writer's pen, or a charioteer's whip.

BOOK ELEVEN

1 · Here are the characteristics of the rational mind: it looks at and delves into itself, molds itself to its own liking, enjoys the fruit it bears (unlike the fruits of the plant and animal kingdoms, which are harvested by others), and completes its mission at whatever point life ends. In a dance, play, or similar performance, the whole action is incomplete if the curtain is suddenly brought down, but the work of the rational mind is complete and whole at whatever moment it is interrupted, so that it can say, "I'm in complete possession of all that is mine."

What is more, the rational mind surveys the form of the whole universe as well as the void beyond. It reaches into eternity and welcomes and understands the universal cycle of rebirth, observing that our fathers saw nothing more and our children will see nothing new. Due to the uniformity of all things, the man who lives to be forty, if he has any sense at all, will have seen everything that was or will be.

Another characteristic of the rational mind is love of one's neighbor. It is also honest and modest at the same time as prizing itself above everything else (which is also a characteristic of the law). From this it follows that the character of reason and justice is one and the same.

2 · You will lose your enthusiasm for singing and dancing and sporting events if, in the case of song, you separate each sound the voice makes and ask yourself, "Am I enchanted by this?" You would be ashamed to admit it. Or in the case of dance, break it down into discrete movements and pauses. Do the same with sporting events. In general, except in the case of virtue and virtuous acts, remember to divide everything into its component parts and to find disenchant-

ment in analyzing them individually. Apply this approach to life as a whole, too.

3 ʼ How lovely the soul that is prepared—when its hour comes to slough off this flesh—for extinction, dispersion, or survival! But this readiness should result from a personal decision, not from sheer contrariness like the Christians, and manifest itself deliberately and soberly, in a convincing manner, without histrionics.

4 ʼ Have I acted unselfishly? Then I have benefited. Hold fast to this thought, and keep up the good work.

5 ʼ What is your job? To be good. How can you do your job without making a careful study, first of nature, then of the peculiar make-up of mankind?

6 ʼ Drama, in its original form as Tragedy, showed us the things that actually and necessarily happen in this life. It reminded us not to panic when we see on the larger stage of life what we enjoy seeing in the theatre, where we recognize how much is unavoidable and how even those who cry "O Cithaeron, Cithaeron" are able to carry on. These dramatists have also given us some useful sayings, such as:

> Though the gods turn their backs on both my sons and me,
> For this too there is a reason.

Also:

> With mere happenstance be not angry.

Or:

> Our lives are harvested like ripe grain.

And many more like these.

After Tragedy came outspoken Old Comedy lecturing us like a schoolmaster and warning us against vanity by means of plain, unvarnished speech. Diogenes, who borrowed from these writers, spoke plainly for the same purpose.

Consider the aims of the Middle Comedy that came later, as well as of the New Comedy that followed and little by little degenerated into a technically clever mime show. No one will deny that these writers say a few useful things, but what is the overall aim and intent of their poetry and drama?

7 · Plainly, no situation is better suited for the practice of philosophy than the one you're now in.

8 · A branch cut from another branch is also, of necessity, cut from the whole tree. Just so, a man estranged from another man is separated from the rest of humanity. But whereas a branch is cut away by someone else, a man cuts himself off from others through his own hatred or neglect, not realizing that at the same time he is cutting himself off from the whole of civilized society.

Thanks to Zeus, the creator and preserver of society, there is a remedy. It is possible for us to grow back together with our neighbor and to contribute once more to the whole. But frequent separation makes it increasingly difficult for the severed part to rejoin the whole and regain its original vigor. Generally speaking, the branch that is grafted on after having been broken off is not the same as the one that grows up with the tree and breathes with it from birth. As the gardeners say, the graft belongs to the tree but doesn't share its thoughts.

9 · If those who stand in your way cannot turn you from the path of reason and stop you from doing what is right, why should they be able to prevent you from treating them kindly? Stand guard in both respects: be tough-minded in thought and action while being gentle to those who oppose or annoy you. It is as much a weakness to become

> STAND GUARD
> IN BOTH RESPECTS:
> BE TOUGH-MINDED
> IN THOUGHT AND ACTION
> WHILE BEING GENTLE
> TO THOSE WHO OPPOSE
> OR ANNOY YOU.

harsh as it is to shrink from action and relent out of fear. Both alike abandon their posts: the one who panics, the other who is estranged from a natural brother and a friend.

10 ' Nature is never less than art, for the arts are simply copies of natural things. This being the case, how can the perfect and overarching nature of the universe be any less artistically skilled? In all the arts, it is the vision of the greater that inspires the manufacture of the lesser, and so it is with nature. From this fact springs justice, and from justice all other virtues trace their roots. We cannot be just when we are distracted by lesser things or deceived by them into making rash or fickle judgments.

11 ' You are all worked up chasing after this and trying to avoid that. These things are not coming to you, so to speak, but you are going to them. Stop desiring the one and fearing the other, and they will stay where they are, and you will not be seen pursuing or fleeing them.

12 ' The soul remains a perfect sphere when it neither pushes out after something nor shrinks back into itself, neither expanding nor contracting, but shining with a radiance by which it sees the truth of all things as well as the truth inside itself.

13 ' Does a man ridicule me? That's his business. It's my job to make sure that nothing I say or do deserves to be ridiculed. Will he hate me? His business again. Mine is to remain gentle and well disposed toward everyone, ready to show even this fellow the mistake in his thinking, not in a scolding tone or with a show of forbearance, but graciously and genuinely like Phocian of old (if he wasn't being facetious). This disposition should come from within, and a man should never be seen by the gods harboring resentments or complaints. What harm can come to you, as a man bent on making this world a better place, if you do what is in keeping with your own nature and accept what is opportune for the whole of nature?

14 ' With hearts full of hate, they fawn on one another. Devising ways to crush their opponents, they bow before them.

15 · How false and beneath contempt is the man who says, "Let me be perfectly frank with you." What is he up to?

There's no need to dress up the truth. It will be evident in your words. Written on your face. Ringing in your voice. Flashing from your eyes—as you understand at a glance the meaning in your lover's look. The sincere and good man gives off such an unmistakable odor that whenever he walks by you can't fail to smell him, whether you want to or not.

Studied sincerity is a stiletto. The wolf's friendship for the lamb is a trap. Avoid these above all. Goodness, sincerity, kindliness—the eyes betray these qualities. They cannot be counterfeited or disguised.

> STUDIED SINCERITY
> IS A STILETTO. THE WOLF'S
> FRIENDSHIP FOR THE LAMB
> IS A TRAP. AVOID THESE
> ABOVE ALL.

16 · The power to live an exemplary life resides in the mind, so long as the mind remains indifferent to the things that are themselves indifferent. But how can it remain indifferent? By carefully examining each thing, both as a whole and in its parts, and by remembering that nothing can oblige us to form an opinion of it. Things don't force themselves upon us. They stand still, while we form judgments of them and write them down, so to speak, on our minds. Yet nothing compels us to write them there, and if by chance we make an unthinking judgment, we can erase it immediately. This mental discipline, remember, will last only a short time, and then life will be over. So why complain and wish it were otherwise? If it is in accord with nature, then rejoice, and life will be easy for you. If it runs contrary to nature, then look for what suits your own nature and strive after that, without worrying about what others may think. After all, no one can be blamed for seeking his own good.

17 · Ask of everything: Where did it come from? Of what is it made? Into what is it changing? What will it be after it has changed? Change will not harm it.

18 · Some considerations when others offend:

First, consider the nature of your relationship to others. We are made for one another. Or from another perspective, I was born to lead, as a ram leads the flock or a bull the herd. Or—returning to the original premise—if not unthinking atoms, then intelligent nature governs everything, and the lower orders of creation exist for the higher, and the higher exist for one another.

Second, what are they like at the table, in bed, and elsewhere? Above all, what actions do their opinions compel them to perform? To what extent are their actions motivated by pride?

Third, if what they do is right, you have no reason to be offended. If wrong, then it's plain they act out of compulsion and ignorance. Just as no one is willing to be denied knowledge of the truth, no one is willingly deprived of the power to treat others as they deserve. Are men not resentful if they hear themselves spoken of as unjust, insensitive, greedy, or in any way nasty to their neighbors?

Fourth, like them, you often do wrong yourself. Even if you refrain from doing certain types of wrong, your character is still bent that way, and only cowardice, fear of what others will say, or some other vile motive holds you back.

Fifth, you have no proof that they are doing anything wrong. Many things are done for reasons that are not apparent. A man must know a great deal before condemning another man's behavior.

Sixth, when you are overwrought with anger or impatience, think how fleeting this life is and how soon you and your vexations will be laid out in the grave.

Seventh, it isn't what others do that troubles you. That is on their own consciences. You are bothered by your opinions of what they do. Rid yourself of those opinions and stop always assuming the worst—then your troubles will go away. How do you get rid of your opinions? By reminding yourself that you aren't disgraced by what others do. For unless only what brings disgrace is wrong, then you too are as guilty as a thief, and worse.

Eighth, our rage and lamentations do us more harm than whatever caused our anger and grief in the first place.

Ninth, as long as it's genuine and without condescension or pretense, kindness is irresistible. What can the most insolent man do if you remain relentlessly kind and, given the opportunity, counsel him calmly and gently even while he's trying to harm you? "No, my son. We are not created for this. I can't be hurt in this way, but you are hurting yourself." In a discreet and roundabout manner, point out to him that bees and other animals by nature gregarious do not act like this. Let there be nothing ironic or scolding in your tone, but speak with true affection and with no residue of resentment in your heart. Don't lecture him. Don't embarrass him in front of others. But address him privately even if others are present.

Commit these nine observations to memory; accept them as gifts from the Muses; and while you still have life, begin to live like a man. Avoid with equal caution flattering others as well as losing your temper with them. Both tear the social fabric and lead to trouble.

To ward off anger, keep these maxims handy:

- There is nothing manly about petulance.
- Because they are more natural to our species, qualities like courtesy and kindness are the more manly. These qualities, not irritability and bad temper, bespeak strength and fiber and manly fortitude.
- The freer the mind from passion, the closer the man to power.
- Anger is as much a proof of weakness as grief. Both involve being wounded and giving in to one's wounds.

And if you like, take this tenth gift from Apollo himself, the leader of the Nine Muses: To expect the wicked not to sin is sheer lunacy. It asks the impossible. Similarly, to allow them to sin against others but not against you is both irrational and surpassingly capricious.

> OUR RAGE
> AND LAMENTATIONS
> DO US MORE HARM
> THAN WHATEVER CAUSED
> OUR ANGER AND GRIEF
> IN THE FIRST PLACE.

19 ' Be vigilant in guarding against four temptations of the mind, and when you detect them, shun them by saying to yourself:

- ' This is an idle speculation;
- ' This will sow discord;
- ' This isn't what I really think (for not to speak your mind begs the question of whose mind you're speaking);
- ' This will lower my estimation of myself.

Lest the divine part within you surrender to the base and mortal part and be forced to feed the coarse appetites of the flesh.

20 ' Although your breath and all the fiery elements in you have a natural tendency to rise, they keep their place in the complex blend of bodily elements in the interest of a well-ordered universe. Likewise, the watery and earthy elements in you want to descend, but they rise up instead and remain in a position that is not natural for them. In this way, even the elements obey the universe and do not abandon their posts, but remain at them, under orders, until the signal sounds for their release once again.

Is it not then disconcerting to discover that only the rational element in you rebels and wishes to abandon its post? Nothing is asked of it except what accords with nature. No violence is threatened or done against it. Yet it refuses to obey and runs away as fast as it can. Its flight toward unjust and undisciplined behavior, toward anger, grief, and fear is nothing other than a flight from nature.

And when the mind resents anything that happens, then too it is quitting its post. It is made for holiness and reverence toward God no less than for justice toward men. These virtues, because they engender in us contentment with the way the universe is ordered, are even older and more important than justice.

21 ' "A man whose aim in life is not singular and consistent cannot be one and the same person throughout his life." But to say only this, without defining what his aim should be, is not enough. Except in the case of those things they hold in common, most people cannot agree on a definition of what is good. For this reason, it makes sense to aim at the common good, the well-being of society

as a whole. He who strives to achieve this aim in life will be consistent in his behavior and therefore one and the same person throughout his life.

22 · Remember what happened to the country mouse who got mixed up with the city mouse—his terror and flight.

23 · Socrates called popular beliefs bogeymen to frighten children.

24 · At festivals and games, the Spartans placed seats in the shade for their foreign guests while seating themselves wherever they could.

25 · Socrates declined an invitation from Perdiccas with these words: "To avoid coming to a dishonorable end," by which he meant, to avoid being treated well without having the power to do good in return.

26 · The writings of the Ephesians contain this maxim: Have before you at all times the icon of an ancient who practiced virtue.

27 · Look up at the sky before dawn, advised the Pythagoreans, and meditate on the constellations that are constant in their relations with one another and unswerving in their duty—orderly, pure, and naked (for no star wears a veil).

28 · They remind us of Socrates in his underwear after Xanthippe ran off with his clothes, and recall what he said to his friends as they blushed and retreated, embarrassed to see him dressed this way.

29 · You can't master the arts of reading and writing until you've studied them. This applies even more to those who would master the art of living.

30 · "Born a slave, what need have you of speech or thought?"

31 · ". . . and the heart in my bosom laughed."
(Homer, *Odyssey* IV.413.)

32 ⸱ "They will accuse virtue and scourge her with harsh words."
(Hesiod, *Works & Days,* 185.)

33 ⸱ "Looking for figs in winter is fool's work. So is wanting a child in old age."
(Epictetus, *Discourses* III.24, 87.)

34 ⸱ "When kissing your child," said Epictetus, "you would do well to whisper these words to yourself, 'You may be dead tomorrow.'"
Words like these are bound to bring bad luck!
"Not at all!" he countered. "Words that merely describe an act of nature can't bring bad luck. Is it bad luck to talk about harvesting grain?"
(Epictetus, *Discourses* III.24, 88.)

35 ⸱ "The green grape, the ripened grape, the dried raisin, change after change, not into nothing, but into something that is not yet."
(Epictetus, *Discourses* III.24, 91.)

36 ⸱ "No one is robbed of his own free will," said Epictetus.
(Epictetus, *Discourses* III.22, 105.)

37 ⸱ He also said, "We must own an effective technique for giving our assent, and in dealing with our impulses, we must keep them within proper bounds, directed to the welfare of others, and in proportion to the worth of their objects. We must abstain from desire no matter what, and pay no attention to the things over which we have no influence or control."

38 ⸱ "This is not a debate over trifles," he said, "but over whether we will be sane or not."
(Epictetus, *Discourses* I.22, 17–21.)

39 ⸱ "What would you prefer?" Socrates used to ask. "A mind that can reason, or one that can't."
"A reasoning mind!"
"What kind of reasoning mind—healthy or depraved?"

"Healthy!"

"In that case, why don't you seek it?"

"Because we already have it!"

"Then why are you quarrelling and at odds with one another?"

BOOK TWELVE

1 · All the good things you want someday to attain can be yours today. Just get out of your own way. Put the past behind you and the future in the hands of God, and refer every present thought and action to piety and justice. To piety by being happy with the fate which nature crafted for you and equipped you for. To justice by speaking the truth freely and simply and by acting as the law requires and as each situation merits. Don't let the wickedness of other men stand in your way, nor your own misconceptions, nor the opinions of others, nor the sensations of your overgrown flesh. Let each sensing part take care of itself.

Now that you are about to depart this life, ignore everything else and attend only to the guiding light of reason and the inspiring spark of divinity within you. Fear not that life will someday end; fear instead that a life in harmony with nature may never begin. Do this and you will be worthy of the cosmos that bore you and no longer a stranger in your own country, puzzled by common everyday occurrences as if you'd never seen them before and dependent on others for every little thing.

> FEAR NOT THAT
> LIFE WILL SOMEDAY END;
> FEAR INSTEAD THAT
> A LIFE IN HARMONY
> WITH NATURE
> MAY NEVER BEGIN.

2 · God sees the minds of men stripped of their material shells and husks and impurities. With his pure intellect, he touches the very parts that flowed from him into ourselves. Make a habit of doing the same and you will rid yourself of most distractions. Will the man who ignores his fleshly shell waste time fussing with his dress, his dwelling, his popularity—the costumes and stage scenery of life?

3 ' You are composed of three parts: the body, the breath of life, and the mind. The first two belong to you insofar as you must take care of them, but only the third is truly yours. Now, if you remove from your true self, which is your thinking self, everything that others may say or do, and everything that you have said and done, and everything that troubles you about the future, and everything that your bodily shell and animating breath force upon you against your will, and everything that dances round you in a whirlwind of circumstance, then your mind will throw off the chains of fate and empower you to live pure and free, doing what is just, desiring whatever happens, and speaking the truth. If, I say, you remove from your ruling intellect everything you can feel and sense and every consideration of time, whether past or future; and if you make yourself as Empedocles says, "A rounded sphere rejoicing in its own spherical bliss"; and if you train yourself to live the only life you possess, life in the present moment; then you will be able to spend your remaining days free from anxiety, kindly disposed toward others, and at peace with your indwelling spirit.

4 ' Often I marvel at how men love themselves more than others while at the same time caring more about what others think of them than what they think of themselves. For example, what if some god or wise counselor instructed us to give immediate utterance to every thought and design that popped into our heads? None of us would put up with such a regimen for a single day. Is this not further proof that we have a higher regard for what our neighbors think of us than for what we think of ourselves?

5 ' How can the gods, who otherwise ordered all things so well and with goodwill toward men, have overlooked this one thing: how can they have failed to make a way for those who are particularly good, who are in closest communion with the divine, and whose virtuous lives and acts of worship place them on terms of intimacy with the divine—how can they have failed to make a way for these few good men to live again once they are dead and utterly extinguished?

Now, if this is the fate of good men, we can be sure that the gods would have arranged it to be otherwise had it needed to be. If it were just, it would be possible; and if it were in accord with nature, nature would have accomplished it. Therefore, from the fact that it is not so (if indeed it is not so), we can reasonably conclude that it should not be so.

Even you can see that now you are arguing with the gods, and it would not occur to you to do this if they were not completely good and just. Would completely good and just gods unjustly and irrationally overlook a part of the universe they have ordered so well?

6 , Practice also the things you don't expect to master. The left hand, clumsy at most things from inexperience, grasps the reins more confidently than the right because it's used to them.

> PRACTICE ALSO
> THE THINGS YOU DON'T
> EXPECT TO MASTER.

7 , Think of what condition your body and soul should be in when death catches up with you. Think of the shortness of life, the vast expanse of time past and time to come, and the frailty of every material thing.

8 , Look to the underlying cause, stripped of appearances; into the intention behind your actions; and at the true nature of pain, pleasure, death, and fame. See how you manufacture your own discontent; how no one hinders you but yourself; how everything depends on your view of it.

9 , Be a boxer, not a gladiator, in the way you act on your principles. The gladiator takes up his sword only to put it down again, but the boxer is never without his fist and has only to clench it.

10 , See things for what they are, dividing them into matter, form, and intention.

11 , What a wondrous power lies within every man's grasp: to do only what God approves and to accept all that God assigns!

12 ᐧ Don't blame the gods for what happens, for they never do wrong either voluntarily or involuntarily. Don't blame men either, whose wrongs are all involuntary. Be done with blame.

13 ᐧ Only a fool or a stranger on this planet will be surprised by anything in this life.

14 ᐧ Either unavoidable Necessity and an unchangeable order, or a Providence that hears our prayers, or a wild and uncontrollable storm. If unavoidable Necessity, why fight it? If a Providence ready to show mercy, why not try to be worthy of divine aid? But if an uncontrollable storm, take heart in such heavy seas knowing that you have reason at the helm. And if the seas wash you away, let them wash away your flesh, your breath, and all the rest. Your reason they will not wash away.

15 ᐧ A lamp's flame throws light and does not lose its radiance until it is extinguished. Will the truth, justice, and wisdom within you die before your life is extinguished?

16 ᐧ When someone gives you the impression of having erred, ask yourself, "How do I know that what he's done is wrong?" And if he really is guilty of wrongdoing, how do I know that he isn't already reproaching himself for it and isn't like a man slapping his own face? Wanting the wicked not to do wrong is like wanting the fig tree not to produce a bitter juice in its figs, or babies not to cry, or horses not to neigh, or other inevitabilities not to occur. From someone with such a character, what else can you expect? If it bothers you, find a way of curing it.

> IF IT'S NOT RIGHT,
> DON'T DO IT.
> IF IT'S NOT TRUE,
> DON'T SAY IT.

17 ᐧ If it's not right, don't do it. If it's not true, don't say it.

18 ˙ Look always at the whole. What is it that has made this impression on your senses? Analyze it by breaking it down into cause, matter, purpose, and duration.

19 ˙ It's time you recognized that you have something higher and more godlike within you than that which tweaks your emotions and pulls your strings. So, what's controlling your mind at this moment? Fear, suspicion, lust, or is it some other vile thing?

20 ˙ First, do nothing unintentionally or without some end in mind. Second, make the common good the only end of all your actions.

21 ˙ A little while and you will be nobody nowhere, as will be all the things you now see and all the people now living. All are born to change, to waste away, and to die so that others may be born in their place.

22 ˙ It all depends on your opinion of it, and that depends on you. Choose to renounce your opinion—and you will find yourself, like a sailor rounding the headland, on a calm sea, in a bay without waves.

23 ˙ No act in all the world is harmed by coming to an end when the time for it to end comes, nor is the actor harmed when his act comes to a timely end. So it is with life, the sum of all our acts. When it is time for life to end, there is no harm in this, nor do we think evil of the one who puts an end to the series of acts that make a life.

Nature prescribes the seasons and sets the limits, sometimes through the nature of the individual, as in the case of old age, and otherwise through the nature of the whole universe that keeps itself perpetually young and fit by constantly changing its parts. Now whatever serves the purpose of the whole is always lovely and right. How then can death be a bad thing, for we are not dishonored by what we cannot control and do not seek? Rather, it is a good thing when the end arrives in season and benefits and serves the purpose of the whole. Thus is the man led by God who not only walks in the way of God, but consciously chooses the same ends as God.

24 ＇ Keep these three thoughts handy:

- First, do not act without a purpose or contrary to the demands of justice. All outward circumstance, remember, happens either by chance or by Providence; and you can't argue with chance, and you can't haul Providence into court.
- Second, think of how every creature grows from a sperm cell to its first breath of life, and from its first breath to the surrender of its last. Think of the elements which came together to form it and into which it dissolves.
- Third, imagine if you were able to soar above the clouds and look down upon the whole scope of human affairs how trifling they would seem in relation to the vast expanse of space and the hosts of heaven. No matter how often you took flight, you would see the same things, so monotonous, so fleeting. What grounds for pride are these?

25 ＇ Jettison your cargo of opinion, and you are saved. Who prevents you from doing this?

26 ＇ Whenever you lose your temper or become upset about something, you're forgetting that everything serves the purpose of the whole, that another's wrong is not your concern, and that whatever causes you to be upset has always happened and will always happen and even now is happening everywhere. You are also forgetting that what binds humankind to one another is not blood and family ties, but the community of mind. You're forgetting too that everyone's mind is of God and flows from the same divine source. You can claim nothing as your own. Your child, your body, your very soul come from God. Finally, you're forgetting that everything is what your opinion makes it and that the present moment is all you have, to live and lose.

27 ＇ Think continually of those who flew into a rage over something, or of those who were celebrated above all others for their

fame, their bad luck, their implacable hatred, or some other extreme. And ask yourself, where are they all now? Smoke and dust and a tale—or not even a tale.

Fix in your mind an example of every kind: Fabius Catullinus on his farm, Lucius Lupus in his gardens, Stertinius at Baiae, Tiberius at Capri, Velius Rufus, or any other whim pushed by pride to an extreme. How worthless is everything so wantonly pursued! How much more worthy it is to take what comes, like a philosopher, and use it to do justice, show temperance, and obey the gods without affectation, for the pride that makes a show of piety is the most perverse pride of all.

28 ⸱ To those who ask, "Where have you seen gods, and how can you be so sure of their existence that you worship them?" I reply: First, they are clearly visible to the eye; and second, I've never set eyes on my soul, yet I honor it. So it is with the gods: I see their power at work around me every day, and I conclude that they exist, and I worship them.

29 ⸱ If you would preserve your life, look thoroughly into everything—matter and cause—and see it for what it is, and do what is just, and speak what is true with every fiber of your being. What else remains but to experience the true joy of living by stacking one good deed upon another and packing them so tightly that not the slightest chink appears between them?

30 ⸱ The light of the sun is one, even when it is interrupted by walls, mountains, and a myriad other things. Being is one, even when it is dispersed among a host of individual bodies. Life is one, even when it is distributed to countless natures, each with its own idiosyncratic limitations. Mind is one, even when it appears to be divided.

Now all the parts of these wholes, whether made of breath or matter, may be unaware of their affinity with one another and held together merely by the unifying grip of gravity. But the mind is powerfully attracted to and combines with what is like it, and the instinct for human fellowship will not be denied.

31 ⟩ Why do you want to go on living? Is it to feel more, to desire more, to grow more, or less? Or is it to be able to continue to talk and to think? What makes any of these things worth longing for? If you conclude there is little value in these, then why not pursue reason and God? Your pursuit will only be undermined by prizing things of little value and fearing that death will rob you of them.

32 ⟩ What an infinitesimal fraction of time's fathomless abyss is assigned to each of us! An instant, and it flickers out in eternity. What a speck in the plenitude of being we are! What a crumb in the bounty of life! How tiny on this broad earth the clod we crawl upon! Be mindful of all this, think nothing important except to do what your nature directs and to endure what the universal nature sends.

33 ⟩ Are my guiding principles healthy and robust? On this hangs everything. The rest, whether I can control it or not, is but smoke and the gray ashes of the dead.

> ARE MY GUIDING PRINCIPLES
> HEALTHY AND ROBUST?
> ON THIS HANGS EVERYTHING.

34 ⟩ Nothing will help you learn to despise death more than the reflection that even those who think pleasure is good and pain evil, yes, even they scorn death.

35 ⟩ Death holds no terrors for the man who calls good whatever happens in due season, who cares more that his acts are reasonable than that they are many, and to whom it matters not whether his view of the world is long or short-lived.

36 ⟩ Man, you have been a citizen of this great World-City! Whether for five years or fifty, what does it matter? Its laws are the same for all men. What grounds have you to complain? You are not banished from the City by a tyrant or an unjust judge, but by the same nature that settled you in the City. You are no different than the actor

who is dismissed from a play by the director who hired him. "But I have played only three acts, not five!" Well said, but your life's drama is complete in three acts. He who once caused your composition and now calls for your dissolution determines the moment of completion. These are not your decisions. Make a graceful exit then, worthy of the grace you have been shown.

SUBJECT INDEX